WILDERNESS CHALLENGE

Grand Canyon's Deer Creek Falls gives youthful explorers a thunderous shower bath.

BOOKS FOR WORLD EXPLORERS
NATIONAL GEOGRAPHIC SOCIETY

Contents:

Young Blood Indians relive the wilderness adventures of their ancestors on a trail ride into Canada's Rocky Mountain foothills.

COVER: *Side trails deep in Grand Canyon offer rocky challenges.*

Copyright © 1980 National Geographic Society
Library of Congress CIP data: p. 104

1
It's Climb Time in the Rockies!

*Story and photographs
by Annie Griffiths*

"It's fun to climb a mountain, but hard work too," says 14-year-old Brian Farris. Using his ice ax, he pulls himself closer to the summit of Colorado's Castle Peak. Spring has come, but snow still covers the mountaintop. At the time, Brian was attending Aspen Middle School in Aspen, Colorado. There he and 11 classmates took an outdoor education course in mountaineering skills. Guided by three instructors, the class climbed three days to reach the top of Castle Peak.

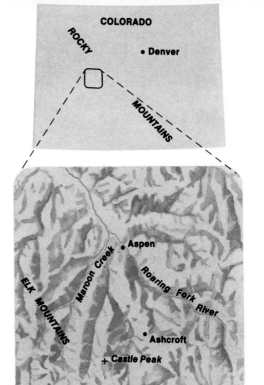

*C*astle Peak rises in the part of the Rocky Mountains called the Elk Mountains. The resort town of Aspen, Colorado, lies near its base. Castle Peak reaches 14,265 feet (4348 m) above sea level. It is the highest point in the Elk Mountains. At a shelter, climbers leave boots in the afternoon sun to dry.

"Being here is such a strange feeling," said Robin Cotton, 13. Robin and eleven of her classmates were beginning a climb up Castle Peak in Colorado. "I feel so small next to this huge mountain," she said. We looked up and could barely see the snow-covered summit. Castle Peak rises 14,265 feet (4348 m) above sea level. The highest mountain in Colorado rises only 168 feet (51 m) higher.* We felt a lump in our throats. Could we do it?

Our adventure was just beginning, but we had prepared for the trip in an outdoor education class at our school, the Aspen Middle School of Aspen, Colorado. Most of us had never climbed in snow before. Our teacher, Mike Flynn, showed us basic mountaineering skills and spelled out some safety tips.

"The normal reactions of your minds and bodies might change as you climb," Mike said. "The higher you go, the less oxygen there is in the air. Because your body needs oxygen, you might have to breathe harder or your heart might have to beat faster as you climb higher. And you might even have trouble thinking clearly."

In late May, the day came for us to start. We piled into two vans and followed a road to a trail. Then we backpacked to a hut to spend the first night. Mike and two other teachers, Scott Edmondson and Dick Hansen, guided us. Wrapped in layers of clothes, we looked like stuffed penguins. Each of us carried a 40-pound (18 kg) backpack containing food, equipment, and clothing.

Until we reached the snow, the hiking was easy. Our packs seemed awkward but not too heavy. The sun warmed us, and melting snow from above filled a nearby creek with icy water. After a while, we crossed the first snowfield. If you have ever walked in deep snow, you know how tiring it is. You sink with each step. Now imagine walking in three feet (1 m) of snow with a heavy pack on your back! The leader had the hardest job because there were no tracks to follow. We took turns leading; in the wilderness, everyone must work together for the good of the group.

"I didn't realize how hard it was to break trail until I did it myself," said Robin. "I had one of the steepest parts. I couldn't give up. I just had to do it."

Up and up we went. Along the way we saw where snow slides had happened. In spring it is dangerous to climb here in the afternoon. As the temperature rises, snow begins melting high on the mountain. Sometimes chunks of snow and ice break loose and roll down the mountainside. To avoid this danger, we stopped climbing about one o'clock each day. By that time on the first day we had reached the hut, about 3,000 feet (915 m) from the top of Castle Peak. Every muscle ached as we ate lunch, but we didn't care.

Later that afternoon we did sit-ups and push-ups. We checked our pulse rates. Many of us discovered that our hearts were beating somewhat faster than they had back in Aspen. Then we remembered what Mike had told us about our minds and bodies working harder the higher we climbed.

*Metric figures in this book are given in round numbers.

*T*he sun rises at base camp (above) nearly 1,000 feet (305 m) below the top of Castle Peak. "The sight of the sun coming up made me want to stay here forever," said Jim Kelley.

*W*et boots dry in the sun (below). Every day the students greased their boots to protect them from the snow.

*Y*eccch! Jim Kelley, Tim Clark, and Jeff Scott, all 14, try their first bites of freeze-dried beef stew (left). "We didn't stir it long enough when we added the hot water," said Tim, making a face. "So it was kind of crunchy."

7

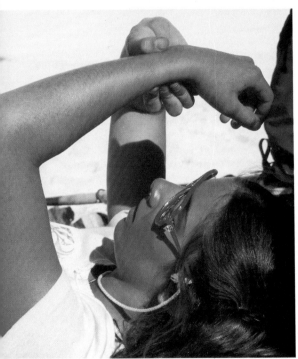

*A*fter running in place, Meg checks her pulse rate. "The higher you go, the less oxygen there is in the air," says Mike. "Sometimes this makes you breathe harder and your heart beat faster. It might even keep you from thinking clearly."

*I*nstructor Mike Flynn holds a watch up to a mirror to see how fast Stacey Adams, 13, can read its reflection. Tim and Jim time her. Such tests during the trip showed how bodies and minds reacted to higher elevations. How quickly can you read the time in the reflected watch Meg Hewey, 15, is holding (right)?

The next day Scott woke us at five a.m. Everyone grumbled about having to get up early. We greased our boots to protect them from the wet snow and covered our faces with suntan lotion. Even though it was cold, we could still get sunburned. We wore sunglasses to protect our eyes. Mike had warned us that the snow is very bright because it reflects sunlight. If we went without glasses, the light would damage our eyes.

As we climbed, we passed the tree line. At higher elevations, trees can't grow because it is rocky and the weather is cold. The going was difficult. "Although we only had to hike half as far as the first day, it was harder because it was steeper," said Meg Hewey, 15. Less than 1,000 feet (305 m) from the summit, we found the perfect spot to set up base camp.

In the afternoon, we talked and wrote notes in our diaries. As the sun grew hot, some snow suddenly broke loose and tumbled down the mountain with a roar. Mike knew where avalanches were likely to happen and always placed our camps out of danger.

That evening we all sipped hot cups of cocoa. Mike said, "Do you know how high we've climbed already? The spot where we sit right now is higher than the highest point in 43 states."

We grinned at each other.

"And here's something else. I'll bet you are at a higher elevation right now than anyone else your age in the whole United States!"

8

*S*tudents learn about a lifesaving climbing tool—the ice ax (above). Mountaineers use the ax to stop themselves from sliding down a slope if they slip. Here instructor Scott Edmondson shows the class the wrong way to stop a slide. In this position, the force of the slide could tear the ax from his hands.

*S*woosh! Beth Madsen, 15, slides past Mike on a snowy slope (right). He hands her an ice ax. She will flip onto her stomach, dig her ice ax into the snow, and stop her slide. All students practice this technique in a safe spot before tackling the final icy stretch to the top.

Our grins widened in pride. It was true! While other kids were at home doing homework or washing dishes, we sat huddled on a mountainside. We had sunburned noses, chapped lips, and sore feet, but we felt as high as a dozen kites! Tomorrow we would climb higher yet. Tomorrow we would head for the summit.

Nobody had trouble getting up the third morning. We ate quickly and hurried off to practice skills we had learned in class. Up to now we were able to climb without using any special equipment. But to reach the very top of Castle Peak, we would need to use ice axes and ropes. Our teachers showed us the correct way to use the ice ax to help stop sliding in case of a slip on a steep *(Continued on page 13)*

*I*n early morning, Mike leads the group across a snowy valley between two peaks. A snow slide of the previous afternoon marks the area. In spring, snow sometimes breaks loose in chunks and roars down the mountainsides as it melts in the hot sun. For safety, the group stopped climbing by one o'clock each day.

10

*A*lmost there. Nearing the summit, Beth rams her ice ax into the snow (above). The ax steadies her as she climbs. "The snow was deep and you had to concentrate on every step," said Beth. "It was tiring, but I wanted to see the view from the top."

*T*ough spot. Mike checks a special knot that secures Stacey to a fixed line (right). The knot slides along as she climbs, but if she slips it tightens immediately and holds her. "I was kind of scared," said Stacey. "I was doing fine, but when I got near the top I got cold feet, not just from the snow! But I kept thinking, 'I can do it.'"

*L*ike a line of ants, the student climbers inch their way up the side of Castle Peak. The steepest part of the climb lies just ahead, where rocks stick through the snow.

"We made it!" shouts Kelsey Stevens, 14, as she reaches the top. "When we had to leave, I didn't want to go."

Grinning from ear to ear, the students and their teachers sit happily in a pile on top of a conquered mountain. "I wouldn't trade this for an 'A' in math," says Stacey.

(Continued from page 9) snowfield. "It's fun to practice using the ax, but serious, too," said Jim Kelley, 14. "It might save your life."

When the instructors were sure we could use the ice ax correctly, we began our final climb. "It's icy in this spot," Billy Madsen, 14, called back as he crossed a slope. Then came Stacey Adams, 13. She took a few steps, then slipped. As she started to slide, Stacey flipped onto her stomach and dug her ax into the snow. Her training paid off. She stopped sliding. She was safe!

Usually at steep points we roped ourselves to an instructor on secure ground above. Then if we slipped, he would act as an anchor to keep us from sliding. In this way, we inched upward. Near the top, the mountain rounds off, like a dome in the sky. We all joined hands and walked the last 30 feet (9 m) together. When we stepped onto the summit, cheers rang out. "We did it!"

"Below us is the whole world," someone said. "Above is nothing but sky." We gazed at nine mountain ranges and parts of three states. "It's fantastic," said Cecily Garrity, 14. "No cars, no noise. Everything is beautiful."

2
New England Kayak Adventure

*Story and photographs
by John Eastcott
and Yva Momatiuk*

"I love kayaking. It is so different and wild out on the river," says Rebecca Dandrow, 11, of Schenectady, New York. Here, she shoots through the Pontook Rapids of the Androscoggin River near Errol, New Hampshire. This was a high point for Rebecca and nine other young people. During a five-day course, they worked with an instructor to learn the skills needed for kayaking.

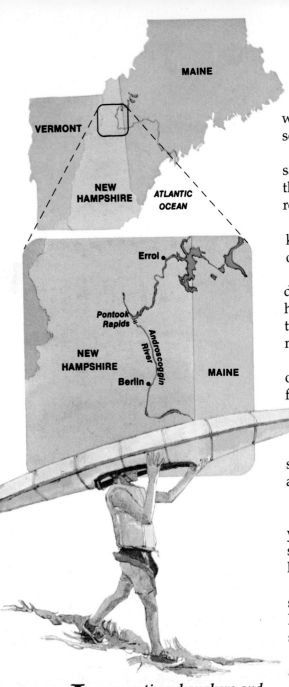

In summertime, kayakers and canoeists of all ages come to the Androscoggin (say an-droh-SCOG-in) River. Many attend courses in boating skills. In some places, river runners must portage, or carry, their craft around rapids. The Androscoggin River flows through parts of New Hampshire and Maine.

Imagine going down a wild river in the north woods in a boat just big enough to fit into! The current is fast. The water turns white with foam. The noise is deafening. The boulders seem to jump at you, especially in rapids, the fast parts of the river.

"When you shoot the rapids, it's like riding a roller coaster," said Jennifer DeCloux, 16, after paddling through a rocky stretch of the Androscoggin River. "You are scared of the boulders. The waves reach as high as your shoulders. They cover the whole boat."

But the little boat can take it. It is a kayak (say KY-ack). Modern kayaks are copied after the Eskimo hunting craft. Kayaks are covered on top to help keep water out.

Jennifer, who lives in Manchester, New Hampshire, had paddled kayaks before. But the Saco Bound/Northern Waters School had its rules. The instructors did not allow Jennifer or the others in the group to enter the rapids until they learned about basic techniques, safety, and equipment.

For their first lesson, the kayakers sat in their boats in a meadow. Here Doug Armstrong, the head instructor, took over. Doug is a former member of the United States Whitewater Team. He explained that helmets should be worn in white water. Life jackets and spray skirts must be worn at all times.

A spray skirt is a short skirt that fits around your waist. After seating yourself in your kayak, you use the skirt to cover the opening and keep water from splashing in.

"You don't just sit in a kayak," said Doug. "You wear it."

Jennifer described the feeling. "You step in carefully, using your paddle to balance your boat against the shore. Then squeeze in, sticking your legs almost straight ahead. You want to fit snug so your kayak leans when you lean, and you and your boat are one."

As part of the next lesson, all the kayakers got into their boats on still water. Doug showed the group the basic paddling strokes. Finally Wendy Barry, 16, also of Manchester, New Hampshire, said, "And now we're ready for the white water!"

But not quite. The shape of the kayak makes it easy to guide, but also easy to tip over, or capsize. "Before you kayak in rough water," said Doug, "you must learn how to 'swim' the rapids. This is in case your boat capsizes. Keep your feet downstream ahead of you, lean back, and tread water with your arms. Don't try to stand up; your foot might get caught between rocks. Once you learn to swim rapids you won't worry about upsetting."

"But how do you get out of a capsized kayak?" someone asked.

"No need to panic," Doug said. "Wait until you are completely upside down, release the spray skirt, and push yourself out of the boat. Swim up, grab your kayak, and hang on if you can. Tow the boat ashore, keeping it upside down. We call this a 'wet exit.'"

Later, in rough water, Peter Merchant, 15, of Norwich, Vermont, accidentally overturned. He quickly surfaced—wet, but alive and well. "It's funny," he said. "The first time it happened, I felt

*D*ry and safe in a meadow by the river, the class begins learning the dos and don'ts of kayaking (left). Doug Gordon, one of the instructors at the school, wears a spray skirt. It spreads out to cover the opening of the kayak when he gets into his boat. This keeps water from splashing in, as it might in an open canoe.

*A*mong lily pads in still water, the kayakers practice paddling (left). "In a forward stroke, one arm pushes and the other pulls," says Doug Armstrong, the head instructor. "Press your feet against the brace inside the kayak and pump your legs with each stroke for more power."

*P*eter Moore, 12, helps his sister Ellen, 14, empty her boat (above). They live in Holliston, Massachusetts.

really scared, but when I slipped out of my kayak and came up for air, I suddenly felt safe. I said to myself, 'I've made it, I can get out anytime I overturn!'"

The next day brought the challenge of the Eskimo roll. Once considered a trick of experts, the Eskimo roll is the only way to recover after an upset without leaving your boat. Now kayakers try to learn it before they run white water. "There are three things to remember when you turn upside down," Doug said. "First, stick your paddle out of the water and slap the surface with it. Second, sweep the paddle across the surface in an arc. Third, press your knee against the side of the boat. Slap, sweep, knee. It's harder to explain than to do. But once you learn it, you'll never forget it."

In shallow, calm water, Wendy Barry, 16, of Manchester, New Hampshire, practices the Eskimo roll. Later, if she overturns, she will know how to right herself without leaving the kayak. (1) Wendy rolls her kayak to the right as Doug Armstrong stands by to help if needed. (2) Under water and upside down, Wendy thinks hard and remembers

Wendy found the technique fascinating. "It was incredible being upside down and looking up through the water and seeing my paddle and kayak. At first I was confused, breathless, hating the water that got in my ears. I kept trying the moves. Slap, sweep, knee. Suddenly it worked. I made everybody laugh, I was so happy. I did it! I wanted to do it again and again."

During breaks, the young boaters played kayak polo by batting a tennis ball back and forth with their paddles. At other times, they scooted through rapids on inner tubes. They went ashore to pick berries. They fought marshmallow battles by the campfire.

Toward the end of the week, the group was ready to go downstream and take what the river had to offer. They knew the trip would be fun, and they would feel safe, because they had practiced the skills necessary for white-water kayaking. Time went by quickly. The river runners learned all about white water. They looked for chutes, where water flows rapidly through narrow passages. They

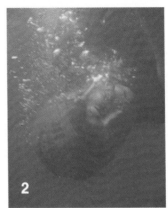

Doug's instructions. Slap the surface with the paddle. Sweep the blade across the surface. Press the knee against the side of the boat. (3) Wendy begins her sweep without Doug's help. (4) Timing pays off. Wendy rolls up, her shoulders and head rising last. "Water got in my ears," Wendy says. "But I love the roll." By coming up on the same side, she did a half roll. "Once you have mastered a half roll, a full roll is nothing," Doug says.

Every sense alert, Peter Moore grips his double-bladed paddle. He is practicing the scull, a stroke that pulls the kayak sideways. Without taking the blade from the water, Peter is moving the paddle in a side-to-side motion that moves the boat to his left. He can do the same stroke on his right.

Youngsters play kayak polo on Aziscohos Lake (right). Trying to swat the tennis ball back and forth improves their balance, Doug told them.

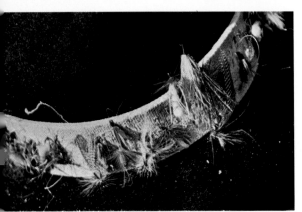

Henry Allain, who lives in Errol, shows the young kayakers how to make flies—(upper). Each fly imitates an insect that fish eat. Each one hides a fishhook. When not in use, the colorful flies decorate Henry's hat band (lower).

bounced over haystacks—the big pointed waves in rapids that look like they are standing still.

Finally, they tried the slalom run. This was a marked course set up by the instructors in swift rapids. Pairs of poles, hanging from wires stretched across the river, formed gates to go through. The kayakers ran the course again and again, sometimes upsetting, sometimes not. On her last run, Jennifer took a small tape recorder sealed in plastic. Here is what she heard later on the playback.

"I am going into fast water now. Paddle hard . . . sweep . . . ferry through gate 4. Straighten up, quick! Ouch! Hit the pole. O.K., I'm fine through gate 5, and here I am in the eddy behind gate 6 which leads across this wicked heavy water to gate 7, and I know I can't make gate 7! I have to angle sharp and paddle hard. I'm going . . . I'm going . . . paddle hard, hard, hard, sweep, sweep, sweep. Whoopee! I've made gate 7!"

The river held no more fear, only challenge and joy.

David Ryan, 14, of Clifton Park, New York, paddles between poles while working his way down a slalom (say SLAH-lum) course (left). This is a water version of the slalom event performed by skiers on snow slopes. The poles hang from wires stretched overhead. They form gates that David must pass through in a certain order in the shortest time possible. Missing a gate or hitting a pole adds penalty points to his score. "It's a great feeling to be alone against the river," David said after a successful run. Under Doug's watchful eye, Melissa Ryan, 13, tests her skills on the slalom run (right, above). "I love to slalom," she says. "Doug tells me that after I go through a gate my eyes light up!" Melissa is David's sister.

Melissa comes up smiling (right). She got an unexpected dunking while learning a technique called ferrying—using the current to help cross the river.

23

3
Trail Ride
to Canada's
Mountains

Story by Judith E. Rinard

Photographs by
David Falconer

"What a great trip for my first horse ride!" said Max Boutland, 10, of Fort Macleod, Alberta, Canada. Max moves single file with other riders across a grassy plain at the foot of the Canadian Rockies. Later, in the mountains, the young American Indians camped on the Blood Indian Reserve, a wilderness area in Alberta. They spent four days riding and exploring and reliving the time when their ancestors rode swift horses across the plains.

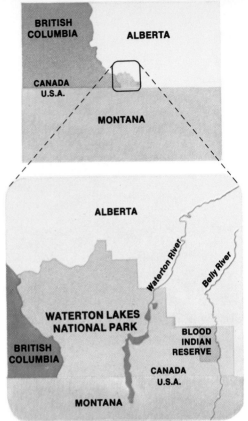

The Blood Indian Reserve and the Waterton Lakes National Park lie in southwest Alberta, Canada. Trails lead horsepackers across valleys and streams into hills and forest-covered mountains. Before starting out, riders load each horse carefully, pulling the straps tight to keep the packs from slipping.

Laurie Tail Feathers, 11, lives in Standoff, a town in Alberta on the plains of western Canada. From his home, he can see the peaks of the Rocky Mountains.

Laurie is a Blood Indian. All around him lies the homeland of his people. The plains and hills once rang with the hoofbeats of thousands of Indian horses. But Laurie seldom rides a horse, and he had never gone on a long trail ride until recently.

Then Laurie and other Indian children got the chance of a lifetime. Rufus Goodstriker would lead them on a horse-packing trip to the mountains. Rufus was once chief of the Blood band of the Blackfoot nation. Now he directs the band's youth program.

"I like to teach the young ones what life was like for our people," said Rufus Goodstriker.

"We'll learn how to ride better and how to get along in the wilderness," said Laurie. "Also we'll learn to track animals and find wild plants we can eat, just as our people did long ago."

The group met on a flat plain near the foot of the mountains. Rufus helped the seven young Indians load food and gear on the pack horses. He showed them how to saddle their own riding horses. He saw that everyone was mounted properly. He adjusted the stirrup straps to match the length of each rider's legs.

"You can't ride a horse right if the stirrups that your feet go into are either too long or too short," said Rufus. "And another thing. Always mount from the left. That's what the horse is trained to expect. It might kick you if you don't do it the correct way."

At first, the ride seemed easy to Laurie. "It was very flat," he said. Then, quickly, the group came to the Belly River, at the foot of the mountains. The trail crossed the river.

The water didn't look deep, but Rufus said there were deep holes in the middle. "We must swim the horses across. Don't panic and pull on the reins," Rufus said. "Just let the horses swim. When a horse swims, it stretches its neck far forward. If the rider pulls back on the reins, it could pull the horse's nose underwater. Then both horse and rider could drown."

One by one, the horses stepped into the river. Each rider lifted boots high and held on to the saddle horn. Soon, the horses reached the deepest water and began swimming toward the other side.

"It was great to feel the horses swimming," said Ruby Coon, 14, of Glenwood, Alberta. "The water was really deep in one part of the river. It came up to our saddles." Because the water flows down from the mountaintops, it is icy cold.

"At first, I was kind of scared," said Max Boutland, 10, of Fort Macleod, Alberta. "But after we made it across, I wanted to go back in and do it all over again. I felt like a young brave on a hunting party of long ago."

The group rode higher into the mountains and through forests. Rufus pointed out a plant growing along the trail.

"Look at this," he said. "It's called kinnikinnick. In the fall, the

As if for a hunting party of old, horses wait to be roped and saddled on the first day of the ride.

berries get red and ripe, and you can eat them. Long ago, our people also used the leaves to make medicine and to smoke in their pipes."

Indians used many other plants for medicine, Rufus explained, as he stopped to show the riders wild licorice, wild rose, and buffalo berry plants. In the old days, people boiled the roots and leaves of these plants to make tea, Rufus said. "We drank the tea to cure the stomachache. And we smeared crushed buffalo berries on a cut to stop the bleeding."

For the next several hours, the riders followed the trail over hills and across grassy plains. The horses stayed in line, one after the other. The group finally reached a campsite that Rufus often used. It was an open space beside a creek. Everyone pitched in to unload the horses and set up camp. Rufus had brought along a tepee for the girls to sleep in. "In the old days," he told the group, "we made tepee covers from the skins of animals, but now we use canvas."

Rufus put a red rag on top of one pole. "Our people believe the rag will keep owls away," he said. "We believe owls bring bad news."

After setting up camp, everyone went down to the creek to

"We saddled our own horses," said Rochelle Goodstriker, 13, of Cardston, Alberta. Here, she, Max, and Ruby Coon, 14, of Glenwood, Alberta, struggle to lift their gear. Once their ancestors rode without saddles.

27

*O*n a trail into the mountains,
Indian guide Rufus Goodstriker
shows the riders how to find wild
plants for food. Rufus encourages his
sons Charlie, 15, and Leon, 11, to
sample kinnikinnick berries. Ruby Coon
and Laurie Tail Feathers, 11, of
Standoff, Alberta, join in the tasting.

*A*fter reaching camp, Ruby hobbles,
or ties, the front legs of a horse
to keep it from wandering away at night
(left). "We only hobbled two horses,"
said Ruby. "The rest stayed nearby
because horses like to stick together.
Hobbling makes it hard for a horse to
run, but allows it to graze."

*G*uide Jim Nielsen helps Charlie, Rufus, and Max pull up the long poles of a tepee (above). Ruby, Laurie, and Rochelle unfold the canvas cover. Rochelle and Michelle Louis, 15, of Vernon, British Columbia, finish pulling up the canvas (right). The tepee served as the girls' sleeping quarters each night. The boys slept in tents.

wade in the cold water, to fish, and to explore. Along the muddy creek bank, Leon Goodstriker, 11, discovered animal tracks.

"These are moose tracks," said Rufus, looking carefully at the size and shape of the prints. "The points of the hooves are too sharp and too close together for an elk."

Soon, it was time to make dinner. Rufus told the campers to gather wet clay from the creek bed. He showed them how to mix the clay with water to make a thick paste. With it they covered fish and placed them in the hot coals of the fire to cook.

"Many years ago," Rufus explained, "Indian hunters cooked their fish this same way. Usually, they also carried pemmican to eat. Pemmican is a high-energy food made of dried meat mixed with fat and crushed berries."

Before going to bed, everyone gathered around the campfire. Rufus beat a small deerskin drum and sang in the Blackfoot language. The song was like a chant.

"This is a song to the horse spirit," he said. "Long ago, our people believed that everything was sacred—the animals, the trees, the rocks, everything. And they believed that the spirits of all these

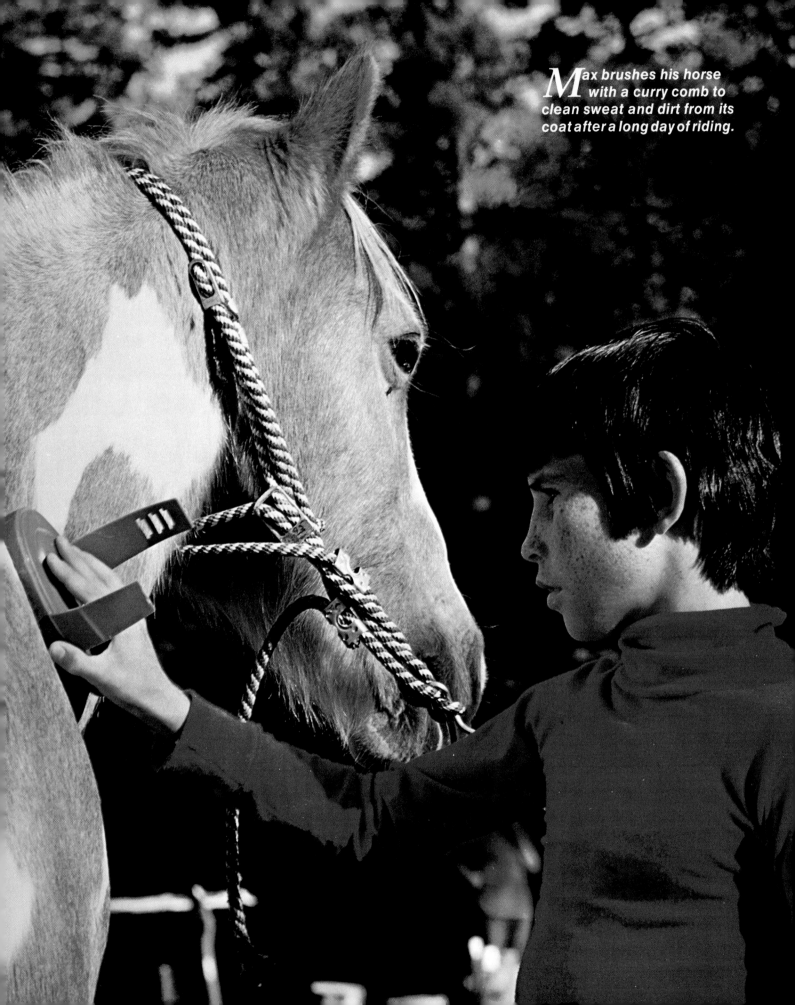

Max brushes his horse with a curry comb to clean sweat and dirt from its coat after a long day of riding.

Hoofprint marks the track of an elk. Indians long ago learned to recognize the tracks of animals they hunted.

This print belongs to a coyote. The riders found the best animal tracks in the soft ground near watering places.

Rufus and Ruby study animal tracks near a creek. "These are elk tracks," said Rufus. "You can see by the size of the prints and the distance between them that it's a large animal. This one looks very big, maybe 900 pounds (410 kg)." Rufus wears a bear-claw necklace. The eagle feather in his hat tells that he was once a Blood Indian chief.

things would listen to our prayers. Tonight, I want to thank the horse spirit for bringing us here today."

Rufus told how, long ago, his people had to walk whenever they moved camp. Dogs carried some things, but women and children had the heaviest loads. Then, like an answer to a prayer, horses appeared on the plains. Tribes to the south had brought them to Blackfoot country, all the way from Mexico. Horses were introduced in Mexico when soldiers brought them from Spain. Before that, Indians in North America had no horses.

Rufus sang again, and told other stories and Indian legends. "Do you know about Bigfoot?" asked Ruby.

"Yes," answered Rufus, "our people believe that big ape-like creatures live in the mountains. We call them Sasquatch, fur people. I've heard many stories. One man, a Cree Indian medicine man, said he saw a huge figure that came near his campfire and then disappeared. He said it looked about nine feet tall."

Everyone shivered for a moment. But as they listened to the crackle of the fire, the campers grew quiet and drowsy. It was cozy to draw closer to the fire and hear the water in the creek rushing past.

A shooting star caught someone's eye. Everyone looked up and noticed the bright stars. They seemed close enough to touch. Rufus pointed out the evening star. "It's an Indian legend that the morning star and the evening star are brothers," he said softly, "and the sun is their father, and the moon is their mother."

The words were like a lullaby. The campers felt tired and sore from riding, but happy and at home in the wilderness. They had done a lot that day. Tomorrow would bring new adventures.

31

*O**n the last day of the trip, Michelle heads her mare into the
Belly River to begin the ride home. Its colt, three months*

Cupping her hands, Michelle holds a small frog she found near the river. The frog escaped and hopped away. During their trail ride, the campers saw hawks, coyotes, and many other wild animals —but not Bigfoot!

old, tags along. "I love riding and exploring every day," said Michelle. "The trip was so much fun I hated to leave."

Curious pine marten, a member of the weasel family, peers from a branch. Driven nearly to extinction by people in the early 1900s, martens still are rare.

4
Testing Wilderness Skills in Hawaii

*Story and photographs
by Jerry Kramer
and Irene Maruya Kramer*

"I really liked being in the wilderness, even though it was hard work at times," said Zerlina Young, 14, of Kamuela, Hawaii. Here Zerlina and eight other young people camp above the clouds on Mauna Loa. The group spent several days hiking to the top of the 13,677-foot (4169-m) volcano. They climbed the mountain as part of a 24-day course offered by Hawaii Bound, an independent wilderness school based in Honolulu, Hawaii. Guided by experts, the young explorers tested outdoor skills in backcountry on the island of Hawaii.

"W̲e're the only people around, and it's great!" said Clint Bova, 13. Clint lives in crowded Honolulu, Hawaii, but now he was backpacking deep in the rugged Kohala Mountains. "It's as if no human beings had ever been here before," he added.

We all felt the same. There were nine of us, taking part in a wilderness program sponsored by Hawaii Bound. This is an independent outdoor school based in Honolulu. Our course called for 24 days in the backcountry of the island of Hawaii, often called the Big Island. We would backpack in rugged mountains, paddle outrigger canoes along the coast, trek across a desert, and climb above the clouds to the top of a volcano.

Our adventure began in the mountains, where we hiked for five days. Most of us had never backpacked before. "Once you got used to carrying 40 pounds (18 kg) of equipment on your back, it was easy," said Stefanie Smart, 14, of Honolulu. "You only had to worry about getting blisters."

Our instructors—Leland Everett and Greg Owen—started right away showing us how to do things. When we set up camp, we each had certain chores to do. Greg pointed out that it was important for us to learn how to work together as a group. "You will face many challenges during the next few weeks, and you'll need to help each other." We called our group *ohana* (say oh-HAH-nuh)—the Hawaiian word for "family."

We all met the challenge of the mountains, then we tackled the Pacific Ocean! We soon learned how much we depended on one another when we braved the surf in an outrigger canoe. This is a special type of canoe with a float that extends a few feet to one side. It is attached to the main canoe by connecting braces. The float helps keep the boat from upsetting in rough water. Our canoes weighed about 250 pounds (113 kg), and that was without loads.

Before we set out in the ocean we practiced paddling in shallow water. "You must work as a team," said Leland. "If the front person paddles on the right side, the second one paddles on the left, the third on the right, and the fourth on the left. If someone wants to change and paddle on the other side, all must change at once." Leland also showed us how to right a boat if it should overturn.

When we were ready, we took to the open sea. As we launched, four to a canoe, Leland shouted: "Remember—pull together!" For the next few days we canoed along the coast. Sometimes we went ashore to investigate the sites of ancient Hawaiian villages, and at night we'd camp on a sandy beach. At first, our muscles ached and our hands got blisters. But each day it became easier to paddle and steer our boats. We were learning to "pull together." "Even though it was hard work," said Brian Fletcher, 15, of San Diego, California, "it sure was a lot of fun."

That was the way we felt about most of our experiences during the 24-day outing—especially hiking in the Kau Desert. The Kau

T̲he state of Hawaii includes eight main islands. Its capital, Honolulu, lies about 2,400 miles (3860 km) southwest of San Francisco, California. The largest island, Hawaii, holds a desert, a rain forest, croplands, beaches, and two volcanoes that erupt frequently. Student explorers rest on a beach in Okoe Bay.

Wearing life preservers, members of the Hawaii Bound group learn to paddle outrigger canoes (below). Hawaiians used these special boats for hundreds of years to travel among the islands. The long float, or outrigger, helps keep the canoe from overturning in rough seas. It takes four people to paddle and steer canoes of this size. "You must learn to stroke together," said instructor Leland Everett. "Otherwise you'll wear yourselves out and get nowhere." In shallow water, the group members practiced righting overturned canoes. They also learned how to handle the boats in a bay before setting out on open water. While traveling along the coast, they stopped to explore small fishing villages. "Paddling was difficult," said Stefanie Smart, 14, of Honolulu. "My arms got tired at first. But once I learned to pull together with the others it became easier."

Clouds settle above Hualalai, a low-lying volcano on the western side of the island of Hawaii (below). It last erupted in 1801, when lava spilled forth, killing all the vegetation in its path. Today plants and trees grow again. The group could see this mountain most of the time.

Stefanie fills her water bottle before setting out across the Kau Desert in Hawaii Volcanoes National Park. The group spent five days hiking through the hot, treeless land. During the trip, everyone drank plenty of liquids to replace the water lost by sweating. In hot weather, sweating helps keep the body from becoming overheated.

Desert is part of Hawaii Volcanoes National Park. It is a hot, almost empty land covered by hardened lava that once spilled out from two nearby volcanoes—Kilauea and Mauna Loa.

Before we set out across this desert, our instructors told us how to keep from feeling sick or dizzy because of the heat. "Don't forget to drink plenty of water," warned Greg. "Your body needs to replace water all the time—especially when it is losing a large amount of liquid through sweating." The instructors also showed us how to use a map and a compass to find our way. We each practiced locating our position. We listened carefully to everything Greg and Leland told us because we were going to plot our own course for a two-day hike through the desert alone.

When the day came for us to set out by ourselves, we were prepared. We carefully picked our way along hardened lava fields that extended all the way to the south coast of the island. From there we hiked to a ranch where Greg and Leland awaited us. The ranch is an old cattle farm that is now part of the park. Here we experienced a different kind of challenge. Each of us lived alone for three days. Our leaders separated us, giving each person an isolated spot for setting up a camp. They also gave us the food we would need.

We found it was hard to be alone that long. Some of us would have welcomed the noise of downtown Honolulu. We made shelters out of rain ponchos, or from fallen limbs and dead bushes. We were not allowed to lose sight of our camp. We saw no one, except for an instructor who came by once each day with fresh water.

"It was awful not having anyone to talk to," said Toby Long, 13, of Honolulu. "Sometimes I got a little bored." "I was afraid of the night," said Zerlina Young, 14, who lives in Kamuela. "So I went to bed before it got dark."

At the end of the three days, our ohana was glad to be back together. We rediscovered the feeling that it's much easier doing things in a group. Now we were ready to begin our last adventure—hiking 18 miles (29 km) to the top of Mauna Loa, one of the world's largest active volcanoes. It last erupted in 1975. Greg told us that the island of Hawaii is actually formed by the tops of five volcanic mountains that rise from the ocean floor.

Zerlina asked when the volcanoes would erupt again. "Scientists don't know for sure," said Leland, "but some people think it will be before the year 2000." "Don't worry," said Greg. "There are special scientists who spend their time keeping track of the volcanoes. We'll get plenty of warning."

It took several days to climb Mauna Loa. The higher we went, the heavier our backpacks seemed to feel. The trail rises a little more than 7,000 feet (2134 m) in elevation. We stopped often to rest and catch our breath. One night we camped in a large cone-shaped hole that was formed by hardened lava. Another time we built a shelter of rocks to protect us from the wind at night.

During the day it was hot, but in *(Continued on page 42)*

*H*ome sweet home. Brian Fletcher, 15, of San Diego, California, pauses for breakfast while building a shelter in the wilderness (above). Brian made his home of grass, leaves, and bark. During the Hawaii Bound course, each member of the group lived alone for three days. "It was a challenge to be by yourself," said Brian.

*S*tefanie uses a rain poncho for the roof of her three-day home in Hawaii Volcanoes National Park (left). To protect her food from rats, she put it in a bag and hung it in a nearby tree.

39

*O*ne by one the hikers trek across hardened lava in Kilauea Iki Crater. Kilauea, one of the most active volcanoes in the world, last erupted in November 1979.

*S*tirring up dust, the young explorers slide down a cinder-covered slope while hiking on the Mauna Loa Trail. They built the shelter of rocks to protect themselves from the cold wind at night. This area was once flat ground. Lava began to spout from a crack, gradually building up this cone-shaped hill. The crater was left when the lava stopped flowing.

*M*olten rock deep inside Kilauea makes underground water boil. The resulting steam escapes through an opening.

*U*sing rope fastened to trees above, Toby Long, of Honolulu, lowers himself down a 90-foot (27-m) cliff (far left). Mountaineers call this technique rappelling.

*B*obie Sue Wilcutt, 14, of Hauula, Hawaii, prepares to rappel down the cliff (left). She wears a hard hat to protect her head. "It's scary," says Bobie Sue, "but the instructors made sure I was safe."

*H*elping hands push Halii McKenney, 15, of Honolulu, toward the top of a barrier at base camp (right). After Halii reaches the top, he will help the others. The group worked together and called itself ohana—*the Hawaiian word for "family."*

(*Continued from page 38*) the evening the temperature dropped to around freezing. Finally we reached the summit. "This was the roughest adventure of all," said Mervin Napeahi, 15, of Honolulu, as he climbed up the last ridge. "It was all uphill!" He was laughing and panting hard at the same time. Later, Zerlina said, "It's beautiful up here at night. You can almost touch the stars."

Back at base camp, we held a celebration. It was a big Hawaiian feast called a luau (say LOO-ow). First, we dug a cooking pit, lined it with rocks, and built a fire in it. We let the fire heat the rocks, then we scattered the coals and put the fire out before adding the food to the pit. We covered turkey, sweet potatoes, and a Hawaiian root vegetable called taro with banana leaves and slowly cooked it all. Nothing ever tasted any better.

We felt both sad and happy that our adventure was ending. Sad because we would miss our ohana, but happy that we had accomplished so much. "At first I didn't think I'd last the three weeks," said Pinkilani Emerson, 14, of Honolulu. "I ended up doing things I never knew I could do."

"It was great," added Zerlina. "I fell in love with Hawaii because I learned more about it than I knew before. Also, I learned more about myself, and that's important."

Everyone in our ohana smiled in agreement.

5
Georgia Swamp Lures Young Paddlers

Story by Charles H. Sloan

Photographs by Rick Perry

"I would like to live like this for about a year," said Bennie Morton, 13. But he and 13 other young canoeists had to be satisfied with a few days of wilderness paddling. All are students from Paideia School in Atlanta, Georgia. They got a good taste of outdoor life while exploring the Okefenokee Swamp in southeast Georgia. In safe places, their instructors allowed them to remove life jackets, but told them to keep the jackets always within reach. Here the waterway is quiet and safe.

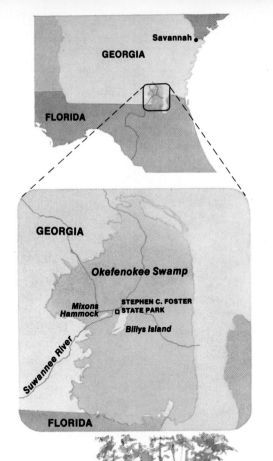

The map shows:

GEORGIA

Savannah

FLORIDA

GEORGIA

Okefenokee Swamp

Mixons Hammock

STEPHEN C. FOSTER STATE PARK

Billys Island

Suwannee River

FLORIDA

Okefenokee Swamp spreads a sheet of water about half the size of Rhode Island across southeast Georgia. Wilderness Southeast, Inc., a nonprofit outdoor school of nearby Savannah, Georgia, operates trips into the swamp for people of all ages. Many groups visit the swamp by canoe. The Okefenokee extends slightly into Florida. The Suwannee River drains most of it.

What is the best thing about paddling through a swamp in a canoe?

"I like the canoeing itself, and I like seeing the reptiles and all the other animals," said Kenny Harris, 12.

"The swamp is a pretty place. It's not as spooky as kid stories make it sound," added Elizabeth Moore, also 12. "Even when we got close to alligators, I was only a little scared."

Kenny and Elizabeth and 12 other young people were exploring Okefenokee (say OH-kee-feh-NO-kee) Swamp in southeast Georgia. All attend Paideia School in Atlanta, Georgia. Students at the school often take trips with an organization called Wilderness Southeast, located in Savannah, Georgia. The main instructor on this trip was Dick Murlless, Director of Wilderness Southeast.

We quickly learned to pay attention to Dick. Even before we put the canoes in the water, he gave us whistles to hang around our necks. "Blow your whistle only if you're in really big trouble," he said. "If you blow and you're not in really big trouble, then you're *really* in big trouble—with me!"

We started from Stephen C. Foster State Park. We loaded all the canoes and paddled single file, two people to a canoe, into a long, wide stretch of water. This was Billys Lake. Here we met our first surprise. Usually "lake" means water surrounded by land. But in the Okefenokee, lakes may be open water surrounded by still more water. The water around such lakes is usually shallow and so thick with grasses and other plants that it may look like dry land. During dry spells, such places may actually become dry land.

"Don't step out of your canoe unless you're sure there is solid land underneath all those plants," warned Dick. "In some places, what looks like land is just a mass of floating plants. Your foot would go right through it. In other places, there is more solid footing, but it's so wet and spongy that it's springy when you step on it. That's how the swamp got its name. 'Okefenokee' sounds like American Indian words that mean 'trembling earth.'"

"Most of the swamp is a national wildlife refuge. The animals and plants own the place," said Cynthia Ocel, an assistant instructor. Dick's wife, Joyce, also an instructor, said, "You won't believe how many animals live here! Opossums, otters, foxes, skunks, bobcats, deer, and wading birds—just to name a few."

For the fun of it, we had grabbed each other's canoes and were drifting along together like a big raft. Suddenly someone spotted an alligator sunning on a fallen tree. The raft of canoes broke apart and everyone paddled to the spot for a closer look. Joyce explained that one way to guess an alligator's size is to estimate the distance between the end of its snout and its eyes. The distance in inches is about the same as the whole alligator's length in feet. "I'd say this one is about seven feet (2 m) long," said Joyce.

The alligator didn't move. "You see, Cynthia is right," Joyce continued. "The gator knows he owns the swamp."

*L*oading up, Beth Holland, 12, takes her pack from Stephanie Cone, also 12 years old (left). The container behind Beth holds part of the group's water supply. Before putting the gear in the canoes, everyone had a chance to practice paddling in quiet water. Some of the group had previous canoeing experience.

More paddling and drifting moved us deeper and deeper into the Okefenokee. The swamp water looked like tea. The color comes from water-soaked twigs and leaves, just as tea leaves soaked in water give tea its special color.

Above the water, Spanish moss, a kind of flowering plant, hangs from the trees like scraggly gray beards. It does no harm to the trees. "It's the Spanish moss, more than anything else, that gives the swamp its spooky reputation," said Dick. "That, plus the fact that there is little solid ground to put your feet on."

Soon, we came to some real ground—Mixons Hammock. This is the name for one of the 70 or so islands in the swamp. The sandy soil

*C*anoes cluster at the edge of Billys Lake (above). Trip leaders tell the paddlers about the swamp's animal and plant life. From the cypress trees above them hangs Spanish moss, a plant that is common in the swamp. It lives on moisture and food that it takes from the air and from rain.

47

Drifting silently through a patch of water lilies, Cynthia Ocel and Elizabeth Moore, 12, carefully slip up on a resting alligator (above). The reptile, 10 feet (3 m) long, was one of more than 15 alligators that the group saw during the trip. Cynthia, in the front of the canoe, went along as an assistant trip instructor.

of these islands supports tall pine trees. Under the pines of Mixons Hammock we camped for the next two nights.

After supper, we learned more about discovering the wilderness. Dick explained that most of the time people use their eyes so much that they often neglect their other senses—touch, taste, smell, and hearing. To find out things our other senses might tell us, he tied blindfolds on each of us one at a time. With sight blocked, we had to use our other senses. We were able to identify pine needles because of their piny smell. Palmetto spines felt prickly. Dry leaves and breaking twigs made a crackly sound. Water felt cool and wet.

The game ended with a kind of hide-and-seek with a tree, played this way: While you are blindfolded, your leader guides you away from the campsite and places your hands on a tree. You're told to get to know that tree. So you touch it, guess its size, reach up to

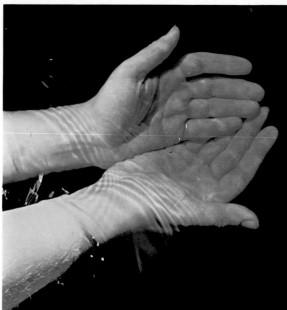

When paddling in for a better look, swamp visitors always leave alligators an escape route. Otherwise the big reptiles, feeling trapped, might rock the boat trying to get away in a hurry.

feel for branches, sniff to see if it has an odor. Then your leader guides you back to the campsite. Off comes the blindfold. You get one more order: "Find your tree!" Surprisingly, everyone does.

All the campers found their tents even more quickly than they found their trees. It had been a full day. Kenny Harris had a visitor near his tent—a raccoon. "It was friendly. It just sniffed around my pack, and then walked away." The night song of frogs and crickets soon lulled everyone to sleep.

Daylight brought a flurry of activity. Joyce and two campers got breakfast going. After eating, other canoeists made lunches and cleaned up. Then the group paddled deeper into the swamp, past tall cypress trees that grow right out of the water. Smaller plants grow almost completely underwater.

"Because so much swamp life is underwater," Dick explained,

The natural coloring of swamp water comes from tannic acid. The acid seeps out of living and dead plants. Tiny bits of dead plants drifting in the water make it still darker. Even in sunlight, you can see only an arm's length into Okefenokee water.

*Y*oung canoeists come ashore on Billys Island in the heart of the swamp (left). The island gets its name from Billy Bowlegs, a Seminole Indian chief who lived in the swamp 150 years ago. More recently, a successful logging town stood here.

*T*his golden silk spider catches insects by spinning a silky web about three feet (1 m) across. The spider's body measures more than an inch (25 mm) long. Joyce Murlless, Beth, and Stephanie found the spider while exploring Billys Island.

"everything has to work hard to find a place to live." He pointed out a caterpillar that burrows into the stems of lily pads. "See," he said, "almost every lily pad has one living in it." It was true. Most of the lilies had a hole down the stem, or bite-shaped pieces missing from the pads. Dick said the swamp also has insect-eating plants. If an insect lands on such a plant, it may be trapped and digested.

Finally we reached Billys Island, one of the biggest islands in the swamp. It takes its name from Billy Bowlegs, a Seminole Indian chief who once lived in the area. If there were such things as ghosts, they might be here—the ghosts of Indians, settlers, and logging crews. People lived on this island for a hundred years. They all are gone now, but a little exploring turned up the rusted remains of a car, some water pipes, and an old water tank. Around 1925, the island held a logging town of about 600 people. The town died when tree-cutting stopped, and people began leaving the swamp to find jobs.

Storm clouds gathered as we turned our canoes into Minnies Run. The water moved so slowly that it didn't seem to be flowing at all. Narrow passages made us stop, then float slowly around the turns, sometimes bumping into trees and other canoes. At the slow pace, someone noticed another strange plant: the neverwet. It sheds water instantly. Again and again we pushed its leaves under the water. Each time they came up dry. The plant sheds water because it has a waxy coating on its leaves.

We wished we had a little waxy coating ourselves as rain spattered across the swamp. The warm shower became a heavy rain, forcing us to turn around and paddle back to Mixons Hammock. The trip to camp was long and soggy.

Now a new outdoors challenge faced the group—starting a campfire with rain-soaked wood. Dick showed how it's done. Everyone who had a knife began scraping bark off dead twigs. The twigs ranged in size from the thickness of a matchstick to the thickness of a grown-up's thumb. The wood under the bark was dry. Soon a small fire crackled. Its heat dried out larger pieces of wood placed nearby.

After supper, we settled down around a roaring campfire. Rain and wetness faded into memories of the past. Next day, we continued through the swamp. Suddenly something plinked against the side of a canoe. Somebody cried out when hit by another something. A battle of the berries had broken out. Everyone seemed to be scooping grape-size berries out of the water and pitching them at everybody else. These were the fruit of the Ogeechee tupelo tree. Some people call this tree the Ogeechee lime. The fruit has a tart, limelike taste and is used in making preserves.

The fight ended as we approached a low man-made dam. Here the Okefenokee, or most of it, empties into the Suwannee River. So we prepared to canoe down the Suwannee, a river made famous by Stephen C. Foster's song "Old Folks at Home." The first lines of the song are "Way down upon the Swanee River, Far, far away." But for us, the Suwannee was here, right at (Continued on page 55)

*C*utting and slicing, Bennie Morton, on the left, and Michael Mermin, 11, prepare lunch for the group. The students took turns cooking and cleaning. For most meals, three campers worked as cooks and three others cleaned up. While the breakfast clean-up crew worked, another crew assembled food for bag lunches. The lunches included sandwiches, fruit, carrots, and gorp—an energy-boosting snack food made of nuts, raisins, and chocolate.

*S*oggy shoes dry beside the fire (left). Leader Dick Murlless told the campers that when the weather is warm, an easier way to dry wet clothing and shoes is to wear them. Body heat does the drying slowly and evenly. Dick is preparing to bake a cake in a heavy metal pot on the campfire. First he heats the lid of the pot in the flames. Then he will put the pot on the fire and heap glowing coals on the lid for extra heat.

*C*alling it a day, 12-year-old Kenny Harris heads for his tent. Flashlights cast a welcoming glow. The students brought their own packs and sleeping bags. The leaders provided canoes, tents, and other gear.

*L*ifting together, students carry a canoe 40 feet (12 m) from the Okefenokee Swamp to the Suwannee River (below). The fully loaded canoe weighs about 180 pounds (82 kg). The students are walking across a low dam that was built to help keep the water at a certain level in the swamp. The river gushes from the swamp through an outlet in the dam. The water in the outlet runs too swiftly for safe canoeing.

*S*pray flying, a canoe skims through shallow waters of the Suwannee River at the end of the trip. Kenny pushes as Thomas Taylor, 13, takes a turn riding the fiberglass canoe.

*D*rifting without a canoe, Caroline Landers, 11, grips a floating boat cushion. After leaving the Okefenokee Wildlife Refuge, Caroline and other campers jumped from their canoes into the cool Suwannee River for a swim.

(Continued from page 51)   our fingertips. It twisted and flowed fast at the beginning, then slowed down.

To get into the river, we carried our canoes across the dam, a broad, grassy ridge of earth. The dam has a concrete-lined outlet that lets water through. The river foams through the outlet so fast that a spill could be dangerous. Once across the dam, we launched our canoes again, all life jackets securely fastened.

We were real pros with a paddle now. We safely reached a slower stretch of the river, and journey's end. During our trip we had learned much about canoeing, about the swamp, and about ourselves. We felt prepared for other adventures in the years ahead.

6
Winter Camping in Minnesota Snow

Story and photographs by Annie Griffiths

Like bear cubs at the entrance to their den, Michael Bridges, 10, left, and 9-year-old Corey Doty peer from a snow shelter. Beside them rests an Eskimo snow shovel. The boys used it to help build their snowhouse. Holding the rope in one hand and the handle in the other allows users to lift large amounts of snow with each scoop of the shovel. Michael, Corey, and ten other young campers learned this trick and other winter wilderness skills during a long January weekend in northern Minnesota. They found that camping in winter can be as much fun as it is in summer.

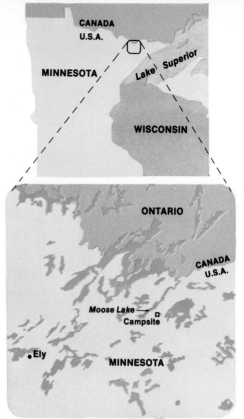

*W*oods and lakes cover much of northern Minnesota, making a year-round recreation area. Boys and girls come to a Boy Scout camp near the Canadian border for canoe outings in summer and skiing trips in winter. From November into April, ice and snow blanket miles and miles of woods and waters. Campers on snowshoes and skis rest near their campsite at Moose Lake.

Dennis Wogaman rubbed his red beard and looked very serious. "We have a saying up here in the north country," he said. "Snow can be one of two things when we go winter camping. It can be our best friend, or it can be our worst enemy. This weekend we will learn how to make snow our friend."

It seemed strange to think of snow as either a friend or an enemy. We were all from the north, but we had always thought of snow as just something to play in or to shovel away.

Dennis went on to tell us how snow can be used as a source of water, for shelter, and as an aid to transportation. "Snow makes the woods much easier to travel through," he said. It was clear that we had a lot to learn about a camping trip in winter!

We had all come from the town of Ely, Minnesota. We would challenge winter by going to a Boy Scout camp called the Charles L. Sommers National High Adventure Base. This camp, near the Canadian border, has a motto it lives up to—that camping should be just as much fun in winter as it is in summer.

Our leader, Dennis, gave us a lot of helpful hints.

"Snow only becomes your enemy," he explained, "when it melts on you! If you are wet and are out in the cold air, you will become cold very quickly." The most important rule for winter camping is: Don't get wet. As a memory aid, Dennis listed the following watchwords for staying warm in winter:

Clean: Keep snow brushed off your clothing. If snow never melts on you, it can't get you wet.

Overheating: Working or playing too hard can cause overheating and perspiration. Getting wet inside your clothing can be worse than getting wet outside.

Layers: Always wear layers of clothing so you can remove or add clothing if you become too warm or too cool.

Dry: Above all else, stay dry when you go winter camping.

Clean, Overheating, Layers, Dry: Put the first letters together and they spell COLD!

Our adventure began on one of the coldest mornings of the year. The temperature was far below freezing.

"It's like living in a deep freeze!" said Jenny Bonde, 14.

Dennis handed out the equipment needed for our trip. We each would carry a sleeping bag made especially for winter camping. In our packs, we would take along a change of clothing and extra socks and mittens in case anything got wet. We began by packing all our heavy cooking gear and all the food on special sleds. We would pull these sleds behind us when we hit the trail.

To get to our camp for the night, we used cross-country skis and snowshoes. Some people call cross-country skis "skinny," because they are longer and narrower than other skis. This shape makes it easy to glide up and down snow-covered trails. Skiing cross-country feels a bit like skating.

Snowshoes look like giant tennis rackets strapped onto regular

58

boots. Snowshoes are very wide and a little hard to walk on. We had to learn how to take long steps with our feet far enough apart to keep one snowshoe from stepping on the other. Using snowshoes, we could walk on deep snow without sinking in.

With all our equipment packed, we set out for our campsite. At first, it was hard to get used to skis and snowshoes. But we soon found that traveling through the woods is easier in winter than in summer, just as Dennis had told us it would be. The snow makes a smooth blanket to glide over. Before long, skiing seemed almost as easy as walking, and it was a lot more fun!

We barely made a sound as our skis cut softly through the powdery snow. Each of us began to feel alone. The woods were as still as an empty church. We heard nothing but our own breathing. Once in a while, bits of snow dropped to the ground from the branches of spruce trees.

The campsite was like a Christmas-card scene. Leaders from the base had worked hard to build a dozen snow shelters. Eskimos and northern Indians sometimes make shelters from snow. Usually they

Before hitting the trail, the campers pack narrow cross-country sleds (below). These sleds slide along easily in the tracks made by cross-country skis. They hold food, kitchen gear, and other heavy items for a weekend camp-out.

With packs on backs and sleds behind (left), young skiers make their way through the woods in below-freezing weather. Rolled sleeping bags look bulky, but they are lightweight.

cut blocks of hardened snow to make an igloo. But here the snow was soft, so the leaders built a different kind of shelter. They lashed branches together, covered them with nylon cloth, and piled snow on top. This made a sturdy shelter of soft snow.

We began building still another type of snow shelter. We used shovels to pile snow into a big mound. We let the mound sit for a few hours to settle and harden. Then we dug into the middle of the mound and hollowed out a space inside. Soon we had a comfortable

*T*eamwork pays off (left).
Combining muscle power
to break firewood are Grant
Doty, 14, Mary Pat Beland, 12,
Jenny Bonde, 14, and Todd
Frisell, 10. Trip leader Dennis
Wogaman had warned against
using saws and axes. Such tools
are especially dangerous in
winter, when cold fingers do not
grip as well as usual.

*T*odd (above) gives a
big squeeze and watches
his water machine in action.
A nylon bag filled with snow
hangs near the campfire. Heat
from the fire melts the snow. A
can catches water as it drips
from the bag. The group uses
the water for drinking and
for cooking.

snowhouse. This shelter also was different from the ones Eskimos make out of solid snow. But it was just as cozy.

Weather predictions called for a cold night, so Dennis decided that we would all sleep in the largest shelter. "You may be surprised to find that body heat does so much to help keep even a large room warm," he said.

We began to gather wood for a campfire. By now we knew that the best way to stay warm is to keep *(Continued on page 65)*

*D*ressed warmly from head to toe, Lisa Melander, 9, straps on her snowshoes (above). "I like using the snowshoes for going into the woods to explore!" said Lisa. These snowshoes are made of lightweight metal and plastic. The northern Indians made them of wood and leather.

*C*ampers in warm sleeping bags listen as Dennis reads to them (right). Stories about explorers of the north seem very real inside this snow shelter. Outside, the wind howls, and the temperature drops to –11°F (–24°C). Inside, the lantern glows and the campers feel snug. A busy day in the cold helps them fall asleep quickly.

(Continued from page 61) moving. Gathering the wood actually kept us warmer than sitting by a roaring fire. We ate supper quickly.

As the sun set, we rushed into our shelter and scrambled into our sleeping bags. Dennis read to us from a book about explorers of the north. Soon sleep overcame two or three of the campers.

A faint sound drifted in from the woods outside. Was it the wind or the evening cry of a timber wolf? As we were falling asleep, the winter woods were waking up. Foxes and mink soon would be prowling the trails we had left in the snow.

We awoke to a frosty morning. Most of us had pulled our boots and clothing inside our sleeping bags to keep them warm through the night. We giggled as we tried to dress inside our snug bags.

After breakfast, we repacked our sleds and backpacks. Again, we slipped silently through the woods on our skis and snowshoes. Back at the base we enjoyed an unexpected snow experience. Ruth Beland, 16, a champion sled-dog racer, had come from Ely to take everyone for a ride. In 1978, Ruth won a gold medal in the three-dog class. In 1979, she took the gold in both the three-dog and the five-dog classes.

For centuries, dog teams have pulled loads for Eskimos and Indians of the north. Today, breeders raise the dogs for racing.

"It's hard to believe that dogs can pull so much weight and run so fast!" said Tani Doty, 12, after her ride.

Dogsledding gave the group one final sampling of the world of winter. We had all discovered how to live with cold and enjoy it.

*S*led dogs, urged on by champion driver Ruth Beland, 16, give Grant a swift ride through the woods.

*T*ani Doty, 12, offers a dog named Choda a hug at the end of the ride. Each camper took a turn in the sled.

7
Backpacking a Yellowstone Trail

Story by David R. Bridge

Photographs by Joseph H. Bailey, National Geographic Photographer

"This country sure makes you feel small," says Fran Bridge, 13. She is backpacking with friends on a trail in Yellowstone National Park. Yellowstone is America's largest and oldest national park, and one of its most popular. Most of its visitors stay close to the paved roads. Fran, of Carmel Valley, California, saw fewer than a dozen other people on the distant trail, although there were thousands of visitors in other parts of the park. "I saw more animals than people," said Fran, "and that was all right with me!"

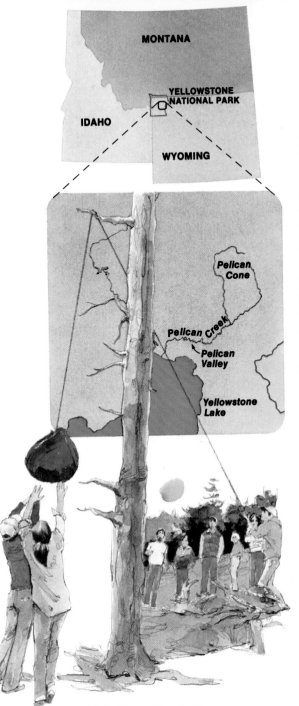

*P*elican Creek flows through a broad valley in Yellowstone National Park. A trail follows it. Young backpackers gathered here to hike a trail and get close to nature. They saw bison, elk, moose, and many smaller animals. At night they put their food in a bag and lifted it out of reach of animals.

"Now I know how a turtle must feel—carrying its home around on its back all the time!"

Fran Bridge, 13, of Carmel Valley, California, was strapping her 30-pound (14-kg) pack onto her back. She and five other young hikers were getting ready for a three-day backpacking trip in Yellowstone National Park.

But the feeling of being a turtle ended quickly as the group started up the trail. Chief guide Andy Shott had seen to it that the packs were placed properly on each back. Shoulders held some of the weight, but the packs also rested on the hips. This transferred much of the weight directly to the hips and legs.

After a few "settling-down" steps, we almost forgot we had packs on. A feeling of freedom took over. Everything we needed we carried with us. It was as if we had cut all ties with the world outside the park. On an inviting trail in the wide-open spaces of the West, we walked freely ahead single file.

We followed the Pelican Creek Trail. Pelican Creek got its name from the big-billed water birds that once nested there. Though we were in Yellowstone, we seemed far removed from its famous geysers, canyons, and waterfalls. In other parts of the huge park, thousands of people crowded to see these sights, while we had the sweet air of Pelican Valley to ourselves.

Well, almost. "Are there any grizzly bears around here?" Deb Schwartz, 13, of Washington, D. C., asked Andy.

"Yes. Bears, along with all wildlife, are protected in the park. Therefore, there're a lot of them. That's why I put those little bells on your packs. They jingle as you walk and warn bears that you're coming. Wild animals can always be dangerous. But it's when you surprise one that you're in the greatest danger."

Thoughts of bears vanished when, suddenly, big banks of dark clouds rolled across the sky. "Looks like rain," said guide Greg Hanchett. "We'd better head for those trees and get out our ponchos and the rain covers for the packs." Within minutes the rain was pouring down on us as we started walking again.

Such sudden storms come and go quickly. In 20 minutes, the sun was shining as brightly as before.

"I'm steaming in here!" said Greg St. Clair, 13, of Red Lodge, Montana, as the sun heated his waterproof nylon rainwear. We stopped at a bend in the trail and put the rain gear away. In the super-clear air following the rain, we looked all around us. A great grassy valley stretched ahead, walled by mountains on the east. We hiked down the middle of the valley for a long time, but we didn't seem to move a bit in relation to the mountains.

Suddenly, everyone was hungry for lunch. "Did we have breakfast this morning?" asked Greg's brother, Kevin St. Clair, 15. "It seems so long ago."

Each hiker, in addition to personal gear, carried one meal for the entire group. We dug the food from one pack and made short work

*C*hief guide Andy Shott, on the right, and Kevin St. Clair, 15, both of Red Lodge, Montana, help Fran into her pack at the start of the trail (left). The pack weighs 30 pounds (14 kg) and holds things Fran will need for the trip. Each member of the group carries some of the food and cooking equipment to help spread the load. They packed heavy items close to their bodies and tucked small things like knives and flashlights in easy-to-reach outside pockets.

of it. Then, putting our packs on again, we hit the trail once more.

"I think I'm getting a blister," said Fran a little later, pulling off one of her boots. Greg Hanchett reached into his pack for a piece of moleskin to protect the sore spot.

"It's good that you stopped so we could take care of it," said Greg. "Blisters are easier to prevent than to cure."

Six and a half miles (10 km) along the trail, we came to our first campsite and found it occupied—by two moose. They looked at us but kept on munching grass while we pitched camp. Guide and cook Leslie Hanchett set up the camp kitchen. Building the fire took time because all the leaves and twigs were wet from the rain.

Greg and another brother, Lee, 16, made an interesting discovery after putting up their tent. "How come it feels so lumpy in here when the ground looked so flat?" asked Greg when he lay down inside the tent.

Down at the creek, splashes of clean, ice-cold creek water on tired, dirty faces revived everyone. Soon, mouth-watering smells began floating on the air as pans sizzled over the fire. The food tasted as it always does around a blazing campfire—good!

The night turned cold. After all, we were almost 8,000 feet (2438 m) above sea level. The sky was so packed with stars that it looked like a sea of twinkling lights. We tied all the food in a big bag and, with a rope, hoisted it into a tree. This was to keep it out of reach of bears and other animals.

One time, in the middle of the night, *(Continued on page 72)*

*"M*ud is a mess!" says Fran when a sudden rain falls on the hikers only two miles (3 km) down Pelican Creek Trail. Such summer storms are common in the mountains.*

*M*unching grass, a bison (above) pays little attention to a yellow tent the backpackers have set up in its grazing area.

*C*indy Hanchett, 9, of Sacramento, California, and Deb Schwartz, 13, of Washington, D. C., help Fran hold up a 6-pound (3-kg) dome tent big enough for all three (left).

*C*indy pretends to be an accident victim. Her father, guide Greg Hanchett, lifts her head to aid her breathing. He sees that she lies on her back to improve blood circulation. The hikers also received advice on what to do for blisters, cuts, broken bones, and snakebites.

The Everts thistle, named for explorer Truman C. Everts, helped save his life in 1870 when he became lost for 37 days in Yellowstone. Eating the root of this prickly plant, also called the elk thistle,

helped Everts survive. Sometimes he boiled the root in one of Yellowstone's hot springs. Many people first learned about the Yellowstone region when Everts wrote an article telling about his "days of peril." Along with his troubles, he described the natural wonders that he and other members of his group had been among the first to see.

(Continued from page 69) Cindy Hanchett, 9, of Sacramento, California, whispered to her tentmates, "I think I hear a bear out there." Nobody wanted to leave the tent to have a look. In the morning, we found tracks on the path to the creek—grizzly tracks, Andy said. But the big bag in the tree was untouched.

After a breakfast of pancakes and bacon, we climbed a nearby hill. There, we learned how to use a map and a compass to find our way in an unfamiliar area. "Oh, I see," Deb said, "all these swirly lines show the shape of the land." "This must be that hill across the valley!" Fran said, reading a topographic map for the first time.

We did not need to plot a course, for we were still following a trail. Our next campsite was also occupied—this time by a large bison. Huge herds of bison once roamed North America. People killed most of them before 1900. Today, bison have increased in Yellowstone and in other public and private reserves.

Pitching camp went more quickly after the practice of the night before. Freeze-dried steaks were the best part of the meal, we all agreed. They looked and felt like pink styrofoam. But after we added water, they looked natural again. With a little mushroom gravy they tasted delicious—just as steaks should!

The chocolate tapioca, on the other hand, failed to jell and tasted as bad as it looked. No one really minded. Lee, Fran, and Deb brought water up from the creek to wash the dishes. They put sand in the cold water to scour the grease off the pans and plates. Then they rinsed them and wiped them dry with a towel.

That night it rained again, a chilly rain, but we were snug in our tents. The next morning, a weasel came out and ran up and down the creek bank looking for food. The weasel stood on its hind legs, then darted into a hole in the bank. On the trail above, a rider appeared leading a string of horses. A lone golden eagle soared across a sky that was beginning to look like winter. Before long, snow would lie deep in Pelican Valley.

"Backpacking gives you a great feeling," said Fran. "You're not just *looking* at things. You're *part* of things."

We struck camp and started the long trek back. Our heads were full of everything this hike in Yellowstone National Park had meant to us. We remembered a sign we had seen at a camp. It said, "Let no one who comes after you have reason to regret that you were here." We followed the simple rule. Like good backpackers, we disturbed nothing and left no trash behind.

On the trail or around camp (right), the guides seldom miss a chance to teach something new. Here, for the benefit of Fran Bridge and Lee St. Clair, 16, Andy compares wild-growing cinquefoil (say sink-foyl) with pictures in a field guide. Cinquefoil, a member of the rose family, has leaves that are divided into five leaflets.

On top of a high hill overlooking Pelican Creek, Greg Hanchett explains a simple method of traveling in the wilderness by using a compass and a special map called a topographic map. The map has lines that show waterways, the shape of the land, and manmade features. You can soon learn to find hills, mountains, and valleys on such a map and match them with the real hills, mountains, and valleys around you.

With a topographic map of the Pelican Valley area and a compass, Fran practices map reading (above). "If that hill over there is this one here on the map, then I must follow this compass course to get there," she says. "The best thing about knowing how to use these tools is that it takes away the fear of getting lost."

At evening, Andy brings out a leather beanbag he calls a "hackey" (right). The campers play a game with it that Andy said was adapted from games enjoyed by North American Indians. Players stand in a circle (above) and try to keep the bag in the air by kicking it. Use of the hands is not allowed. A successful kick to another player is called a pass. The group's record was 14 passes.

8
Wildwater Challenge in Grand Canyon

Story by Paul Martin

Photographs by David Hiser

With the white water of Hermit Rapids foaming around her, Blair Pogue, 14, of La Mesa, California, clings to a wave-tossed boat. She sits in front and to the left of boatman George Gerhart. Ruth Stevens, of Grand Rapids, Michigan, gasps for air beside her. The two young women and 22 other people are exploring Arizona's Grand Canyon in dories. These sturdy boats challenge some of the largest runnable rapids in the world.

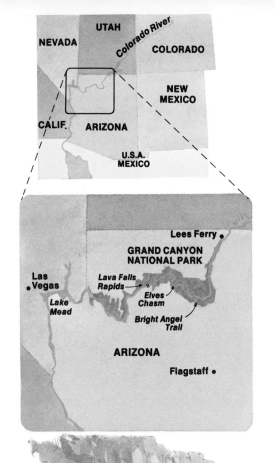

Like a twisting snake, the Colorado River flows through the Southwest. In Arizona it cuts deep into the earth to form the Grand Canyon. The river drops 2,200 feet (671 m) in elevation during the 277-mile (446-km) trip through the canyon. Dozens of huge, swift rapids await modern-day explorers who launch dories and challenge the wild river.

"When you see your first big rapids in the Grand Canyon," said Blair Pogue, 14, of La Mesa, California, "you think 'Oh, no! We'll never make it. There's no way!'

"You feel so helpless. There you are, at the bottom of a canyon a mile deep. You're barreling along the Colorado River as fast as a train, it seems. The waves pile up higher than your head. At the edge of the water, you see nothing but bare rock walls rising almost straight up on both sides."

But Blair quickly found that it's possible to challenge such rapids and come through safely. "You just learn to depend on your boatman," she said.

Blair came to explore the Arizona canyon and its roaring waters with her father, Bill, and her 11-year-old sister, Kirsten. They joined 21 other persons traveling in wooden boats called dories. A type of rowboat 17 feet (5 m) long, the dories were specially designed and built for shooting rapids. Each dory carried a boatman and up to four additional river runners.

Eighteen of the passengers had begun the trip at Lees Ferry, at the northeastern end of Grand Canyon National Park. The rest of us joined them 87 miles (140 km) down the river after a hot hike along Bright Angel Trail. We barely had time to store our equipment in the dories before our boatmen guided us to the middle of the river. Here the swift current pushed us faster and faster. Head boatman Regan Dale, a veteran of 65 trips down the Colorado, called out the rules of the river. "Keep your life jackets on at all times," he said. "Always stay seated. Remember to hold on to the handrails."

Regan also explained what to do if a dory turned over. "It's not likely to happen, but if it does, get out from under the boat. Then make sure the boat is between you and any rocks that you might hit. Don't get trapped between the boat and the rocks. Your life jacket will keep you from sinking."

Suddenly, boatman George Gerhart interrupted Regan with the cry, "White water ahead. This is Horn Creek Rapids!"

We could hear the rapids before we saw them. The water made a low, rumbling sound. The river narrowed as the dories drifted between the high rock walls. Gradually, the dories began to pick up speed. The sound of the water grew louder.

As the boats came around a bend, water sprayed into the air ahead of us. We couldn't yet see what was causing the spray—a series of raging rapids where the river races over rocks and drops suddenly in elevation. The boatmen stood to see what was ahead. Then they sat down and one by one began rowing to a certain spot on the brink of the rapids.

"Our most important job is to get the boat started down the rapids at exactly the right spot," said George. "From then on, it's pretty much up to the river."

We soon saw, and felt, what he meant. The river dropped several feet at the beginning of the rapids. *(Continued on page 83)*

*B*ill Pogue, of La Mesa, California, and his daughters, Blair, 14, center, and Kirsten, 11, hike down Bright Angel Trail (above). The eight-mile (13-km) trail leads to the Colorado River at the bottom of Grand Canyon. The Pogues started hiking at 6 a.m. while it was cool. When they reached the river four hours later, the temperature had soared almost to 100°F (38°C). At the river, the Pogues boarded dories for a two-week adventure on the Colorado River.

*B*lair helps boatman Andre Potochnik wash off his dory with river water (right). Passengers stored their equipment inside the boat's watertight compartments, shown here with hatches open. Each dory carried extra oars to replace any that might be lost or broken.

*S*lapped by a huge wave, Kennet Goldsmith, 12, of Matthews, North Carolina, says hello to the Colorado River (right). Andre Potochnik guides their dory through the white water (above). "I wasn't scared in the rapids," Kennet said, "because I trusted Andre. But the water was really cold."

80

*R*iver runners come ashore and enter Christmas Tree Cave, named for a tree-shaped salt formation. Explorers gave colorful names to many features of the canyon.

*A*ndre shows their location to Blair and Kirsten, rear, and Ann Baker of Mill Valley, California (left). They are hiking in a side canyon that joins the main canyon. Andre uses a special map called a geologic map. It shows the different kinds of rocks in various colors. The boats stopped often to allow time for such hikes.

*E*xploring the narrow canyon above Deer Creek Falls, Blair inches her way down a cliff (right). Tom Collet, of Monte Dourado, Brazil, helps her get good footing. Andre holds a safety rope tied around Blair's waist. The force of rushing, silt-laden water shaped the walls of this canyon thousands of years ago.

(Continued from page 78) Then it rose up in a foaming wave ten feet (3 m) high. The swift-flowing river carried the dories toward this wall of water like small pieces of driftwood. All anyone could do now was take a deep breath and hold on.

With a spray of water, the first dory slammed into the rapids. The dory's bow pointed skyward. Water poured over the side into the boat. In a moment, the boat was over the top of the first wave and racing down the other side. Filled with water, the dory slammed into a second wave, then a third, and a fourth.

In a matter of seconds, the boat had passed through the rapids. When all the dories were safely through the white water, the boatmen called, "Okay, everybody, get the water out! Bail!"

Sitting in the cold water, we all grabbed buckets and bailed furiously. We laughed and talked about our thrilling ride. Nearly everyone had the same feeling—happiness mixed with relief that we had made it safely through.

"When I first saw the rapids," said Blair, "I thought I would be scared. But it all happened so fast and was so much fun that I didn't have time to be scared."

George pointed out that we shouldn't lose our respect for the river. "You need to be frightened sometimes," he said. "The

*J*ane Whalen, a member of the crew, second from left, tells young river runners about prehistoric American Indians. "These Indians lived here hundreds of years ago," Jane said, "and built this rock dwelling (right). Some of them may have spent winters at the bottom of the canyon and summers on the canyon rim." Listening to Jane are Kathy Goldsmith, 14, her brother Kennet, and their cousin Bibi Seiler. Dories float by on the river below.

*K*irsten places her hand beside a handprint from the past. Using white clay, Indians decorated canyon walls with such prints.

important thing is to know when you *should* be scared." During the next two weeks, the dories took us through dozens of rapids like Horn Creek Rapids. These included Lava Falls Rapids, with waves more than 15 feet (5 m) high.

But we didn't spend the entire trip running white water. We had plenty of time to sit back and enjoy the scenery while we drifted on calm stretches of the river. And we stopped the boats many times to explore small side canyons that join the main canyon.

During one stop, we hiked into a small side canyon above Deer Creek Falls. From the river, we could see the waterfall that drops about 100 feet (30 m) out of this canyon's mouth (page 1). Our boatmen became trail guides and showed the way up the steep slopes to the top of the falls. The trail was a series of steep switchbacks all the way to the top. There, we had a sweeping view of the river far below.

From a point above the falls, we hiked back into the narrow canyon. The clear waters of Deer Creek rushed by below us. Our boatmen told us the names of the different kinds of rocks we saw. These often formed colorful bands, almost like the layers of a cake.

Farther along, we found handprints that had been made by ancient American Indians. These Indians had once lived in the Grand Canyon. "They used white clay to decorate the walls of the canyon," said Regan. "They disappeared hundreds of years ago, but we don't know why."

During another stop, we explored Elves Chasm, a fairyland of rocks, water, and plants (cover). There, we hiked past half a dozen small waterfalls on our way to the end of the short canyon. At the top of the climb, we discovered another waterfall that plunged over a steep rock wall and fell into a small pool.

Trees grew all around the pool. Brightly colored wild flowers, ferns, and mosses sprinkled the ground. We were amazed to find so many kinds of plants growing in this rocky world.

Elves Chasm was only one of the surprises that the Grand Canyon had for us. We marveled at the number of animals we saw throughout the trip. Several times we looked up from the boats and saw bighorn sheep on the ledges above the river. While hiking, we spotted many kinds of birds, lizards, and insects.

Each night, the group camped on the sandy beaches along the river. Everyone pitched in to unload the boats and to help set up camp and prepare the meals.

"We all felt like one big family," said Blair. "We always worked together and helped each other through the rough spots."

In camp one evening, the boatmen told us how Grand Canyon was formed. They explained that the canyon was shaped over a period of millions of years. "The river has cut its way down to rocks that are almost two billion years old," said boatman Andre Potochnik. "It is still cutting a few inches deeper every thousand years or so."

Kennet Goldsmith, 12, of Matthews, North Carolina, said some of the cliffs he saw "looked like someone had carved them." Andre

*B*oatman Kenton Grua, left, shows Kirsten, Pita Seiler, 16, and Kathy a boat used by an adventurer named Charles S. Russell. In 1915, Russell gave up his attempt to run the river. Instead, he hiked out of the canyon.

Water splashing over her, Pita (left) cools off under a small waterfall on one of the last days of the trip. Kathy slides down the wet rocks to Pita's right.

Everyone helps load the 450-pound (204-kg) dories onto a truck. The truck will carry the dories back to the beginning of the canyon for another trip down the river.

With a farewell hug, Pita says goodbye to Kenton and to the canyon. "I hated to go," Pita said. "I really loved everything about our trip."

told him that the canyon was cut out of rock by the force of the Colorado's rushing waters. Wind, heat, rain, and ice also helped to shape the walls and cliffs we see today.

"These same forces are still at work here," Andre said. "Over the years, they have cut the canyon to a maximum depth of one mile (1.6 km) and to a width of up to 18 miles (29 km) in one place."

Andre also told us about the early exploration of the canyon by Maj. John Wesley Powell. "Major Powell, a veteran of the Union Army, led the first boat trip down the Colorado in 1869," Andre said. "There were no maps of the river then, so Powell and his party of nine men had no idea what they would find."

What they found was a river so wild that even until 1950 fewer than a hundred persons had dared to travel down it. Today, however, this river trip has become so popular that thousands of people run the Colorado every year.

At the end of their trip, many people find it sad to leave the river. As Blair said, "Running the Colorado begins to become a habit. You just want to keep on shooting the rapids."

9 Enjoying the Wilderness

Exciting adventures fill the previous chapters. Do you think you would like to climb a snow-covered peak or canoe through a swamp? To find out if wilderness is for you, test yourself in a camping and hiking area close at hand—as these backpackers in the drawing are doing. For starters, rent or borrow a tent and a sleeping bag. Don't buy expensive items in the beginning. Gradually build up your own equipment as your interest in the outdoors grows.

...While Remembering the Rules

The important thing is to have fun. But rules are important, too. By following the rules, you can be sure of having fun on your wilderness trip. Learn all you can about the area where you are going. Don't go if bad weather is forecast.

Never go exploring alone. Travel in threes, if possible. That way, if someone is hurt, one person can stay with the injured companion while the third goes for help. It's best if one of the three is an adult.

Always let someone who is staying behind know where you are going and when you plan to be back. If you don't return in a reasonable time, people will know where to start looking for you.

At least one member of your group should carry a first-aid kit and know how to use it. Even on a day trip, pack plenty of food and water. Your appetite may surprise you.

It's nice and cozy around a campfire. But when camping in a park or a recreation area, check the rules before you build a fire. Many places forbid campfires, or permit them only in certain areas. Never leave a fire unattended or go to sleep before it is out.

If you become lost or separated from your group, stay put and let the group find you. Don't start on a hike if you are not feeling well. A serious illness might develop and put you and your group in danger.

Do not feed or tease any wild animal. Some can be dangerous no matter how harmless they look.

If you plan to take a wilderness trip with an organization that sponsors such outings, make sure the organization is reliable. There are hundreds of wilderness groups in the United States and Canada—some better than others.

Carry a good supply of drinking water from home or from a dependable source. If you must drink from lakes or streams, use water-purification tablets to make the water safe. Follow the directions on the bottle when using these tablets.

Do not eat a wild plant unless you know it is safe. Some types of mushrooms, for example, are extremely poisonous.

Plan your trip so that you stop early enough each day to set up your camp before sundown.

Shoes...the Bottom Line

🍁 The young adventurers below know that on an outing nothing gets a harder workout than your feet. Proper shoes are an important part of wilderness wardrobes. The wrong footgear can make you miserable and ruin your trip. This does not mean, however, that you need to go out and buy new shoes every time you go exploring.

🍁 When new shoes or boots *are* needed, choose the right kind for the activity you are planning. Go shopping with somebody who has had wilderness experience and who knows what footwear is best.

🍁 Be sure your shoes fit properly before you leave the store. If they feel tight—don't buy them! You're only asking for trouble.

🍁 When trying on hiking boots, wear two pairs of socks like the ones you would wear on the trail.

🍁 Break in your boots before you set out on a long hike. Wear them often, several hours at a time, until they feel comfortable.

🍁 Remember not to lace your footgear too tightly.

🍁 Before you put your boots on, make sure your feet are in good condition. Clip your toenails.

🍁 Wear two pairs of socks. Many hikers prefer one pair of wool and another lighter-weight pair underneath. Wool absorbs sweat and cushions the feet. Use foot powder to help keep your feet dry.

🍁 Wear only socks that are in good condition. Spots that have been mended or worn thin cause blisters.

🍁 At the first sign of a sore spot on your foot, stop and take care of it.

The rugged hiking boot takes rough, backcountry areas in stride (below). Its high-quality materials, reinforced toe and heel, and interior padding cushion the feet. This makes it more comfortable for backpackers who are carrying heavy loads. A pair weighs about five pounds (2 kg).

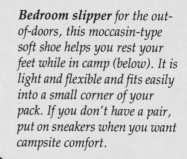

Bedroom slipper for the out-of-doors, this moccasin-type soft shoe helps you rest your feet while in camp (below). It is light and flexible and fits easily into a small corner of your pack. If you don't have a pair, put on sneakers when you want campsite comfort.

Put your best foot forward in a sturdy, lightweight, nonskid trail boot (above). With a reinforced toe and heel and padding around the ankle, this old standby provides enough support for packing average loads over most trails. A pair weighs about four pounds (1.8 kg).

AS YOU HIKE, BE ALERT to any messages your feet may be sending you. A hot sensation on a heel could mean that a blister is forming. Stop, take off the shoe, and have a look. Broken, untreated blisters may become infected.

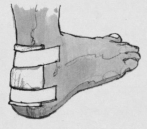

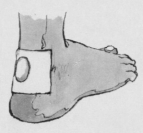

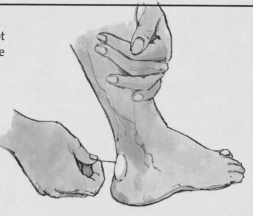

If you have a hot spot, but a blister has not yet formed, wash the foot with soap and water, then dry it. Place a piece of moleskin over the sore area to prevent further irritation. Moleskin is a soft, felt-like padding.

If a small blister has already formed, here's how to keep it from breaking. Wash and dry the area. Cut a doughnut-shaped piece of moleskin and circle the blister with it. This prevents further rubbing.

Drain blisters if you can't protect them from breaking. Sterilize a needle in a match flame. Puncture the blister at its edge. Press out the liquid without tearing the skin. Apply antibiotic cream and a bandage.

Stopping for lunch on a mountain trail, young backpackers enjoy the sun's warmth. They wear two pairs of socks and sturdy boots to cushion their feet on the rocky path. Loose-fitting cotton pants, shorts, and shirts are comfortable on the trail. Cotton or part-cotton material keeps hikers cool during the warm months. Windbreakers, sweaters, and rain ponchos provide extra layers to meet changes in the weather. Dark glasses and caps with bills give protection from the sun.

Clothing ... Layered for Heat and Cold

Before you set out on a long trip, learn about the area you will be exploring and the kinds of weather you might expect. Some places are warm during the day and cold at night; others have frequent rain. It is better to take several loose layers of clothing than one heavy layer. Then you can put on or take off layers as the temperature changes.

Pullover garments are warmer than clothes that button or zip. But garments that open in front allow you to cool off without removing your pack.

In choosing what to pack, consider the weight of each item and the length of your trip. Remember, you

will be carrying everything! You will need fewer items for a weekend than for two weeks in the wild.

Always take lightweight rain gear. A sudden storm can turn the brightest day into a bad experience if you are not prepared.

In the winter, wear wool clothing. Wool is warmer than any other fabric. It holds body heat better than other fabrics, even when it is wet.

Do not wear hoods or scarves that restrict your vision. One wrong step in the wilderness could be dangerous.

92

In the summer, don't depend solely on shorts. Always take along a pair of long pants in case you run into cool weather, insects, thick brush, or a burning sun. If you are planning to hike off the trails in backcountry, wear long pants from the start.

Avoid wearing dangling ties, long belts, or anything that might catch on a bush or a tree and cause you to hurt yourself.

Dress in clothing that allows free movement. It's better for your clothes to be one size too big than to be too small.

In warm weather, clothes made of cotton and part-cotton material are coolest. When the temperature drops, wool garments give the best warmth. Avoid jeans if you expect to be in wet or cold areas. Denim absorbs water quickly and dries slowly.

Before you purchase any clothing, search your attic or closets for family hand-me-downs. You may already have some of the clothing you need. After all, you're going backpacking, not to a fashion parade.

If you must buy, compare prices and quality at surplus stores, discount houses, and outfitting stores.

Hot chocolate warms a young outdoorsman. He and his friend keep comfortable when the temperature drops by dressing in several layers rather than in one bulky layer. They wear long thermal underwear under heavy pants, and a long-sleeved shirt or a turtle-neck sweater. Cool-weather campers wear clothes made of wool or part-wool fabrics, since wool helps the body retain heat. They top their layers with an insulated vest or a jacket (usually filled with down or a synthetic fiber). Gloves and a wool hat complete the outfit. The body loses heat quickly in the areas farthest from the heart. Keeping head and hands covered helps the entire body stay warm. There's an old saying: If your feet are cold, put your hat on.

93

Packs and Things
for Kids and Kings

In the wilderness, your pack becomes your house. It is bedroom, bathroom, kitchen, and living room rolled into one. No one pack is ideal for every person. The one shown here serves serious backpackers on long trips. The tent is rolled like a sausage on top of the pack. Above the hips, straps secure the sleeping bag. Two other types of packs (opposite) may better suit your needs. Check them out with an adult.

A good rule to follow: Carry one-fourth of your weight, including the weight of the pack. Consider the weight of each item. For balance, put the heaviest items high and close to the body. Stow the medium-weight gear in the center. Put light items low and farther from the body. Use common sense; too much gear can be as bad as too little.

Save the outside pockets for your water bottle, first-aid kit, snacks, rain gear, map, and compass. Keep a drinking cup handy. In areas inhabited by bears, tie on a bell that jingles as you walk. Wild animals usually leave if they know you are coming.

HOUSE ON YOUR BACK contains everything you need for a trail hike of several days.

Tent and sleeping bag unroll for a good night's sleep under the stars.

Don't forget toothbrush and paste, insect repellent, sunburn lotion, comb, soap, and toilet paper.

Always carry a compass and a topographic map. Even if you're following a trail, you could get lost.

Carry drinking water in a canteen on your belt or in a plastic bottle in an outer pocket of your pack.

Take an all-purpose knife. Special knives have several blades, a can opener, a screwdriver, and scissors.

Extra clothes include rain gear, socks, jackets, vests, and sweaters. Take soft shoes for comfort around camp.

94

For carrying medium weights, consider the internal-frame pack (below). Narrow in design, it hugs the back, putting most of the weight on the shoulders. Cross-country skiers, mountain climbers, and many backpackers prefer this pack because it gives them greater mobility. It holds a load of up to 35 pounds (16 kg).

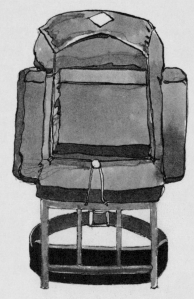

Smallest of the backpacks, the daypack (above) provides enough room to carry a light load on a short hike. Usually made of a water-repellent nylon, the bag has one or two deep compartments. When not in use in the wilderness, the daypack can double as a bag for carrying schoolbooks or for shopping.

Long-distance backpackers use a pack attached to an external frame (above). The frame, made of aluminum, fits the body. It enables an adult hiker to carry up to 75 pounds (34 kg). A padded hip belt at the base of the frame shifts much of the weight onto the hips. Outside pockets store frequently used items.

For cooking and eating, take lightweight pots and pans, utensils, and a cup that doubles as a bowl.

Your first-aid kit includes bandages, tape, moleskin, a needle, a manual, and an emergency whistle.

In areas where you can't build a fire, use a small backpacking stove that runs on bottled fuel.

Freeze-dried foods and powdered milk are lightweight and don't spoil. Take tablets to purify water.

Three kinds of light will see you through: waterproof matches, a flashlight, and candles.

Every camper should carry trash bags, nylon cord for emergencies, and a trowel or a shovel for digging.

And So To Sleep

All campers, even the backyard variety, need to get a good night's rest. Tents and sleeping bags provide comfort, but come in many different sizes and shapes and materials. Select the types best for you, depending on where and at what time of year you plan to camp.

Roomiest to sleep in, the rectangular bag (below) can also be the coldest. Its full size requires more body heat to keep it warm, and makes it heavier to carry. The bag works best in mild weather.

Narrow at the ends, the mummy bag (above) provides the least room but usually gives the most warmth. It is light in weight. A cold-weather hood pulls over the top, leaving only the camper's nose and mouth exposed.

Wide in the middle for elbow and hip room, the semi-rectangular bag tapers slightly at the bottom (above). Its shape makes it warmer than a rectangular bag and allows more movement than a mummy bag.

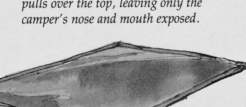

Plastic groundsheet (above), placed under your sleeping bag, gives extra protection from cold or damp ground.

Foam rubber pad, unrolled under a sleeping bag, gives extra comfort. Spare clothing also makes a cushion.

When sleeping outdoors, keeping warm can be a problem—even in summer. One trick is to have as much under you as over you. A groundsheet and a pad help a lot, especially if the ground is cool or damp. Groundsheets are also useful at sandy campsites.

No one sleeping bag is ideal for everyone. If you are planning to buy one, consider its weight, the climate where you'll use it, and your sleeping habits. Are you usually hot when you sleep, or cold? Do you toss and turn and need a lot of room? Will you be sleeping inside a tent or out in the open?

The filling of a sleeping bag helps determine its warmth. Before you buy, read the label and ask the advice of an expert. A filling of down usually gives the greatest warmth, but is expensive. A down bag absorbs water easily and is hard to dry out. Bags filled with fiberfill cost less and are easier to dry, but they're usually not as warm. Select the bag that fits your needs, at a price you can afford.

Always air out your sleeping bag before putting it away. Keep it clean. Store it away from heat and sunlight. Good care will make it last longer.

Camping out is fun—even in your own backyard. And it need not be expensive. To make a shelter, hang a canvas sheet over rope strung between trees. Stake the back corners to the ground. Tie the front corners with cord and stretch the sheet to form an overhang. Need a sleeping bag? Roll up in a couple of old blankets. An old shower curtain makes a fine groundcloth.

Easy to pack and to set up, the lightweight pup tent is a favorite with young backpackers. It requires only two poles, some cord, and a few stakes. Because of its shape, the pup tent has less space than other tents.

Roomier inside than a pup tent, the dome type of tent does not require cord and stakes. Its poles fit into built-in sleeves on the tent. Once campers assemble this tent, they can change its location in the campsite without having to take it apart.

External frame tents have poles on the outside to steady them. This type of tent is easy to set up and is roomy inside. Campers can move this tent without taking it apart.

With a design like the tepee of certain Plains Indians, the pyramid tent has extra head room and more usable space than some other tents. Many campers prefer this design in snowy weather. Snow slides off its sloping roof.

This Spot to Be Saved for Future Generations

A scene like this is worth going a long way to see. And it is worth saving for all the people who will follow you. Practice the tips for good camping on these pages. You will be enjoying, but not destroying, the wilderness.

Don't feed the animals. In some areas, wild animals raid garbage cans and campsites looking for food. For the good of these animals, as well as for your own safety, do not leave your food where animals can reach it. Between meals place your camp food in a sturdy bag. Hang it from a nylon cord strung between two trees or looped over a strong branch. Raise the bag at least ten feet (3 m) off the ground and more than three feet (1 m) from the tree trunk. To avoid nighttime visitors, select a tree far from your tent.

98

Tinder: Use dead leaves, bark, or pine needles to start your fire.

A campfire is a friend, so don't make it an enemy. Before starting one, ask an adult to help. Did you check to see if you are in an area where campfires are permitted? If so, choose a spot away from overhanging trees and grass and clear a circle ten feet (3 m) in diameter. Always set a bucket of water nearby. Place tinder in a pile in the center of the ring, then put kindling on top. Once the fire catches, add firewood. Never cut live trees for fuel. This is destructive and doesn't help your fire, since live plants do not burn well.

Never leave a fire unattended. Before taking a walk or settling down for the night, put the fire out. To douse a fire, let it die down, then pour water on the hot coals. Stir the ashes and pour on more water. Turn any coals and wood still smoldering and sprinkle water on them. When a fire has died completely, the ashes will feel cool to the touch.

Kindling: Add dry sticks and small branches from dead trees.

Fuel: Dry logs or dead branches make fires blaze.

Nothing tastes as good as food cooked over an open fire. To make a fireplace, put rocks on either side of the fire close enough together to hold the pot securely. If you have a grate, use it to rest the pot on. A grate is especially useful if you want to heat more than one pot at a time. When you move on, put the fireplace stones back where you found them.

In areas with no toilets, dig a latrine with a trowel or a small shovel. Make the hole about eight inches (20 cm) deep. Soil breaks down waste matter quickly at this depth. Replace the dirt and pack it down.

So that others may enjoy the wilderness after your visit, leave your campsite in good condition. Carry out all your litter. Replace logs or rocks you might have moved. Make sure all latrine pits are filled. Do not destroy anything—plant or animal—just to have a souvenir. Remember the camper's motto below.

Take only memories…
Leave only footprints.

Wilderness Associations

Are you ready to take a trip of your own? The groups listed on these pages can provide you with valuable information and instruction. Many of the organizations sponsor outings. Others publish books and magazines with information about equipment, safety, and places to go. You can check your phone book for other organizations near you.

American Alpine Club
113 East 90th Street
New York, New York 10028

American Canoe Association
4260 East Evans Avenue
Denver, Colorado 80222

American Forestry Association
1319 18th Street, Northwest
Washington, D. C. 20036

American Whitewater Affiliation
3115 Eton Avenue
Berkeley, California 94705

Appalachian Mountain Club
5 Joy Street
Boston, Massachusetts 02108

Appalachian Trail Conference
P.O. Box 236
Harpers Ferry, West Virginia 25425

Additional Reading

Books on these pages give further information about places to go on a trip of your own. They also tell what kinds of outings are available. The list includes books about wilderness skills and books that tell you how to plan outings. There are even books to take along with you. These are only a few of the many books about wilderness activities. Some of them are inexpensive paperbacks, but others are not. Look for these and other volumes in libraries, bookstores, and most wilderness outfitting stores.

Do you want to know more about the trips and activities in *Wilderness Challenge?* **These books further describe some of the places our young explorers visited and some of the types of things they did.**

Bauer, Erwin, *Cross-Country Skiing and Snowshoeing*, Stoeger Publishing Company, South Hackensack, N.J., 1976.

Bridge, Raymond, *The Complete Guide to Kayaking*, Charles Scribner's Sons, New York, 1978.

Cary, Bob, *Winter Camping*, Stephen Greene Press, Brattleboro, Vt., 1979.

Ferber, Peggy, ed., *Mountaineering: The Freedom of the Hills*, The Mountaineers, Seattle, 1979.

Fisher, Ron, *Still Waters, White Waters: Exploring America's Rivers and Lakes*, National Geographic Society, 1977.

Hillcourt, William, *Official Boy Scout Handbook*, Boy Scouts of America, 1979.

Jacobson, Cliff, *Wilderness Canoeing and Camping*, E. P. Dutton, New York, 1977.

Manning, Harvey, *Backpacking One Step at a Time*, Random House, Inc., New York, 1973.

Merrill, Bill, *Vacationing with Saddle and Packhorse*, Arco Publishing Company, Inc., New York, 1976.

National Park Foundation, *The Complete Guide to America's National Parks*, Washington, D. C., 1979.

Smith, Robert, *Hiking Hawaii: The Big Island*, Wilderness Press, Berkeley, 1977.

Tinker, Gene, *Let's Learn Ski Touring: Your Guide to Cross-Country Fun*, Walker and Company, New York, 1972.

More ideas for different kinds of outings can be found in these books. They also include information about equipment and planning trips.

Cardwell, Paul Jr., *America's Camping Book*, Charles Scribner's Sons, New York, 1976.

National Geographic Society, *Wilderness U.S.A.*, 1973.

National Wildlife Federation, *Wildlife Country: How to Enjoy It*, Washington, D. C., 1977.

National Park Service
U. S. Department of the Interior
Room 1013
18th and C Streets, Northwest
Washington, D. C. 20240

Boy Scouts of America
P.O. Box 61030
Dallas/Ft. Worth Airport, Texas 75261

Canadian Youth Hostels Association
333 River Road
Vanier City, Ottawa, Ontario
Canada K1L 8B9

Ski Touring Council
West Hill Road
Troy, Vermont 05868

Parks Canada
Department of Information
Room 2800
10 Wellington Street
Hull, Quebec
Canada K1A 1G2

Sierra Club
530 Bush Street
San Francisco, California 94104

The Wilderness Society
1901 Pennsylvania Avenue
Washington, D. C. 20006

U. S. Ski Association
The Broadmoor
Colorado Springs, Colorado 80906

Perrin, Alwyn T., *The Explorers Ltd. Source Book,* Harper & Row, Publishers, New York, 1977.

The Reader's Digest Association (Canada) Ltd., *Outdoors Canada,* Montreal, 1977.

A well-planned trip makes the best trip. These books contain tips about equipment, camp cooking, wilderness skills, and things to do on an outdoor adventure.

Barker, Harriett, *Supermarket Backpacker,* Greatlakes Living Press, Publishers, Matteson, Illinois, 1977.

Kjellstrom, Bjorn, *Be Expert with Map and Compass: The Orienteering Handbook,* Charles Scribner's Sons, New York, 1976.

McPhee Gribble Publishers, *Out in the Wilds: How to Look After Yourself,* Penguin Books Australia Ltd., Ringwood, Victoria, 1977.

Sequoia, Anna and Schneider, Steven, *Backpacking on a Budget,* Penguin Books, New York, 1979.

Finally, there are pocket-size books to go with you on your trip.

Trail Guides have maps that show trails, and descriptions that tell you how long and difficult the trail will be. Campsites are shown, as well as picnic sites. You can find the guides in libraries or buy them from the people who maintain the trails.

Field Guides help you identify things you find along the trail and around the campsite. There are guides for plants, trees, birds, insects, reptiles, mammals, animal tracks, rocks and minerals, shells, even stars! Look for guides with information about the area you will be visiting.

Consultants
The Special Publications and School Services Division is grateful to the individuals, organizations, and agencies named or quoted in the text and to the individuals cited here for their generous assistance: Duane Barrus, *Waterton Lakes National Park;* Ann Beck, *Hawaii Bound;* Douglas N. Bernhard, *Wilderness Consultant;* Tim Blank, *Yellowstone National Park;* Dr. Glenn O. Blough, *Educational Consultant;* Jeanine Noel Brumbeau, *Nutritionist;* Chris Cameron, *Hawaii Volcanoes National Park;* Ann Dunn, *Alberta Department of Native Affairs;* Dan Dzurisin, *Hawaii Volcano Observatory;* William T. Endicott, *Coach, U. S. Whitewater Team;* Dr. John C. Ewers, *Smithsonian Institution;* Roger E. Giddings, *Grand Canyon National Park;* Caleb R. Hathaway, *Canoe Cruisers Association of Greater Washington, D. C.;* Judy Hobart, *Librarian;* Gary H. Johnston, *Biologist;* Ray Junge, *Colorado Geological Survey;* Martin Litton, *Martin Litton's Grand Canyon Dories;* Dr. Nicholas J. Long, *Consulting Psychologist;* National Climatic Center, *National Weather Service, National Oceanic and Atmospheric Administration;* Bill Thomas, *Stephen C. Foster State Park;* Yellowstone Wilderness Guides.

Composition for WILDERNESS CHALLENGE by National Geographic's Photographic Services, Carl M. Shrader, Chief; Lawrence F. Ludwig, Assistant Chief. Printed and bound by Holladay-Tyler Printing Corp., Rockville, Md. Color separations by the Lanman Companies, Washington, D. C.; Progressive Color Corp., Rockville, Md.; The J. Wm. Reed Co., Alexandria, Va. *Classroom Activities Folder* produced by Mazor Corporation, Dayton, Ohio.

Index

Bold type refers to illustrations; regular type refers to text.

Wilderness Challenge

PUBLISHED BY
THE NATIONAL GEOGRAPHIC SOCIETY
WASHINGTON, D. C.

Gilbert M. Grosvenor, *President*
Melvin M. Payne, *Chairman of the Board*
Owen R. Anderson, *Executive Vice President*
Robert L. Breeden, *Vice President,*
Publications and Educational Media

PREPARED BY THE SPECIAL PUBLICATIONS
AND SCHOOL SERVICES DIVISION

Donald J. Crump, *Director*
Philip B. Silcott, *Associate Director*
William L. Allen, William R. Gray, *Senior Editors*

Staff for Books for WORLD Explorers Series
Ralph Gray, *Editor*
Pat Robbins, *Managing Editor*
Ursula Perrin Vosseler, *Art Director*

Staff for this Book
Ralph Gray, *Managing Editor*
Don A. Sparks, *Picture Editor*
Viviane Y. Silverman, *Designer*
Nancy J. Watson, *Project Editor*
Barbara Grazzini, *Assistant to the Managing Editor*
Mark Bellerose, Gunn Associates, *Artist*
Sallie M. Greenwood, *Consulting Editor*
Barbara Grazzini, Nancy J. Watson,
    Senior Researchers
John D. Garst, Jr., Jerald N. Fishbein, Gary M.
Johnson, Patricia J. King, Alfred L. Zebarth,
    Map Research, Design, and Production

Engraving, Printing, and Product Manufacture
Robert W. Messer, *Manager*
George V. White, *Production Manager*
Richard A. McClure, *Production Project*
    Manufacture
Mark R. Dunlevy, Raja D. Murshed, Christine A.
Roberts, David V. Showers, Gregory Storer,
    Assistant Production Managers
Susan M. Oehler, *Production Staff Assistant*

Staff Assistants: Debra A. Antonini, Pamela A. Black, Barbara Bricks, Jane H. Buxton, Mary Elizabeth Davis, Rosamund Garner, Nancy J. Harvey, Jane M. Holloway, Joan Hurst, Suzanne J. Jacobson, Artemis S. Lampathakis, Ellen Quinn, Marcia Robinson, Katheryn M. Slocum

Interns: Mary B. Campbell, Richard A. Fletcher, Sara Grosvenor, Kit Pancoast, Margaret J. Tinsley, Phyllis C. Watt, Nancy P. White

Far-out Fun: Mona Enquist, *Project Editor;* Paul M. Breeden (cover art); John Eastcott and Yva Momatiuk (cover photo); Lois Sloan (2, 16, 23); Dan Johnson/Art Direction Inc. (3-6, 15, 18-20); Roz Schanzer (7, 8, 17); Sue Levin (9-14)

Mount Everest Game: Ralph Gray, Barbara Grazzini, Viviane Y. Silverman, *Concept, development, and design;* Barry C. Bishop, Sallie M. Greenwood, *Consultants;* Heinrich C. Berann, *Background art;* Sue Levin, *Superimposed art.*
Poster photo, Annie Griffiths

Market Research: Joe Fowler, Karen A. Geiger, Carrla L. Holmes, Meg McElligott, Stephen F. Moss

Index: Mary Kathleen Hogan

Library of Congress CIP Data
Wilderness challenge.
    (Books for world explorers)
    Bibliography: p. Includes index
    SUMMARY: Relates young people's wilderness experiences with kayaking, mountain climbing, horse packing, swamp exploring, backpacking, winter camping, and white-water running. Includes a wall poster and booklet of games and puzzles.
    1. Outdoor recreation—United States—Juvenile literature—Addresses, essays, lectures. 2. Outdoor recreation—Canada—Juvenile literature—Addresses, essays, lectures. 3. Wilderness areas—United States—Recreational use—Juvenile literature—Addresses, essays, lectures. 4. Wilderness areas—Canada—Recreational use—Juvenile literature—Addresses, essays, lectures.
[1. Outdoor recreation. 2. Wilderness areas] I. National Geographic Society, Washington, D. C. II. Series.   GV191.4.W53   790'.0973   79-3241
ISBN 0-87044-333-X (regular binding)   ISBN 0-87044-338-0 (library binding)